practical
BONSAI
for
beginners

Five needle pine, prepared approximately 150 years ago. This famous plant is roughly two feet tall and is planted in an extremely fine old Chinese vessel. This bonsai is from the collection of Mr. Kosaku Tsukizaki of Tokyo.

practical
BONSAI
for
beginners

by Kenji Murata

Japan Publications Trading Company

Tokyo · San Francisco

Published by
JAPAN PUBLICATIONS TRADING COMPANY
of Elmsford, San Francisco, and Tokyo with editorial
offices at
2-1, Sarugaku-cho 1-chome, Chiyoda-ku, Tokyo, Japan

Available in the British Commonwealth
(excluding Canada and the Far East)
through WARD LOCK & COMPANY LTD.,
Warwick House, 116 Baker Street, London, W1M, 2BB England

© 1964 by Kenji Murata

Translated by
Masatsugu Tsuzawa and Donald C. Mann

Library of Congress Catalog Card Number 64-7611
ISBN-0-87040-230-7

First printing: October 1964   Seventh printing: April 1971
Second printing: March 1966   Eighth printing: June 1971
Third printing: April 1967   Ninth printing: April 1972
Fourth printing: June 1968   Tenth printing: April 1973
Fifth printing: April 1969   Eleventh printing: July 1974
Sixth printing: August 1969   Twelfth printing: June 1976

Printed in Japan

TYPESETTING AND LETTERPRESS BY KENKYUSHA PRINTING CO.
PHOTOGRAVURE BY TOKYOINSHOKAN CO., LTD.

Contents

Preface

BONSAI, *those potted dwarf trees which are a unique and alive Japanese object of art, have become one of the wonders of the world. Potted trees can be found anywhere in the world, but none like the Japanese bonsai, for the bonsai is the achievement of human creative talent.*

Today, although there are several volumes on bonsai available in English, there are very few books dealing with practical elementary bonsai techniques such as SEISHI, *or shaping up, transplantation, and the selection of bonsai vessels.*

Needless to say, the ultimate objective of raising bonsai is the creation of masterpieces. However, no matter how fine a bonsai is, it must be raised from a seedling. Bonsai is truly an horticultural hobby, as its aim is not the collection of fine bonsai masterpieces by offering large monetary remunerations. On the contrary, the pleasure and the satisfaction, which is available to one and all, is the raising of bonsai by oneself, whether it be by means of seedage or a plant obtained from the wilds. I have written this volume with this view in mind, considering it to be a " guide to bonsai," and hopeful that it will prove to be useful to beginners.

In addition to the color photo of a Five needle pine on the jacket, this book contains many other pictures of bonsai masterpieces, some of which have been handed down through the centuries and carefully nurtured by each succeeding generation. It is by no means a simple matter to exert loving care and devote oneself to these masterpieces for years on end without a single day of " rest," whether it rains or shines. Therefore there is good reason that one's efforts are so highly esteemed.

My original intention had been to include many photos of those bonsai which had been cared for by generations of the same family. However, I was unable to do so as this volume is aimed at providing the reader with a very basic knowledge of bonsai.

Rather, I have laid specific emphasis on seedlings, material plants (especially in regard to evergreens), and other pertinent information in order to help the reader understand the basics of bonsai, together with reference pictures and illustrations. I only regret that I found it impossible to include complete instructions in this volume due to the number of species that are involved.

The trees mentioned in this volume are easily obtainable in Japan or abroad, especially in the United States which has so many similar evergreens that are eminently suitable as bonsai material.

In days of old, many Japanese UKIYOE *(woodblock) paintings today considered as extremely precious were sold to France at ridiculously cheap prices. And it was when these same Japanese objects of art were reintroduced to Japan that they suddenly created a tremendous interest among Japanese towards the once-forsaken cultural heritage.*

In the same token, it is quite possible that bonsai, towards which many Japanese are quite indifferent, may come to be highly valued among people abroad and masterpieces by them sent to Japan.

Bonsai being raised abroad today are still in the early stages. But what a pleasure it will be when the day comes that will see a mutual exchange of bonsai between Japanese and foreign raisers.

With the fast onslaught of civilization, the world seems to have grown smaller because of easier accessibility between the different nations. I sincerely hope that the day will come when bonsai lovers the world over will be able to gather together, overcoming national borders and characteristics, and discuss their common hobby—bonsai.

July 1964   KENJI MURATA

Appreciation of bonsai

BONSAI, a living art object, is an artistic piece created with a superb aesthetic sense and dexterity which brings out the full natural beauty of the plant used as the basic material. The "artist" creator of a bonsai plants his material in a small bonsai vessel and with it tries to portray either an old tree atop a mountain or a stately giant tree growing in a vast plain.

There are five essential points which must be considered in regard to the beauty of a bonsai.

1. DEVELOPMENT OF ROOTS

Those roots which spread in all directions and appear to be immovable as they exert a firm grasp on the soil are considered to be very fine examples.

2. TRUNK

A well-tapered trunk with a thick base is greatly appreciated by most people. Then naturally, a bonsai having the appearance of an aged tree is preferable to one that has the looks of a young tree. Particularly prized are those trunks whose bark has slightly rotted, baring the trunk underneath and thereby giving the impression that the tree is hundreds of years old. These types are known as *saba-miki* and *shari-miki*.

3. BRANCHES

The best situation regarding branches is to have the thick branches developing out towards the sides (as in regard to the front or viewing side of the bonsai), with the small branches growing out from the front and rear of the trunk. A variety of branches—thick, thin, long, short—also is desired. *Mikikiri-eda* are those branches that cut across the main trunk as seen from the front of the bonsai; *kuruma-eda* are those which radiate out from one point of the trunk; *kannuki-eda* are those branches which grow out horizontally and in opposite directions from the trunk. These three latter categories are disliked and are not considered appreciable.

4. LEAVES

Leaves should be small, dense and lively. *Himesho* or *yatsubusasho*, or bonsai with densely growing small leaves, are especially highly valued.

5. CORE

The core of the tree, namely the upermost portion of the tree, must show strong vitality which is symbolic of its life. Those bonsai with a broken core or a core which has been cut are not considered to be good. However, the top of a trunk which has taken on the appearance of a skeleton due to natural withering after it has lived a long life is highly valued because it shows a sad tint of natural austerity. This type of core is known as *jin*, or god. Examples of common bonsai figures now will be illustrated with the use of photographs.

PLATE 1. *Chokkan* (Straight trunk). This is a very natural shape featuring a single straight trunk tapering towards its top. If the roots are well-developed, the lowest branches 20% to 30% of the tree's height above the ground, the branches alternately growing to left and right, and the center of the tree properly located, the plant takes on a very stately appearance. (Common Ezo spruce. Age 200 years.)

PLATE 2. *Shakan* (Leaning trunk). This is the single-trunk bonsai with a slight inclination to right or left. This type of tree is often found along the seashore or in mountain areas. (Five needle pine. Age 200 years.)

PLATE 3. *Bankan* (Curving trunk). A single trunk, but bending in four directions, it expresses the strong vitality which has enabled the tree to survive years of natural hardships. (Five needle pine. Age about 350 years.)

PLATE 4. *Sokan* (Double trunk). A single tree with two separate trunks. One should be longer and thicker than the other. Harmony between the two trunks is of utmost importance. (Five needle pine. Age 100 years.)

PLATE 5. *Kabudachi* (Trees in group). From one to more than 10 trees growing in a group. Apart from the first one, the number of trunks always is kept at an odd number, avoiding such even numbers as 2, 4, 6, 8, 10, etc. Small groups are known as *sankan* (3 trunks), *gokan* (5 trunks), and *shichikan* (7 trunks). (Red-leafed hornbeam. Age 80 years.)

PLATE 6. *Netsuranari* (Separate trunks from one root). Trunks of various sizes seemingly growing independently but being connected by one root. The number of trunks varies from 3–5 to more than 10. This is a very unique bonsai shape. (Common Ezo spruce. Age 70 years.)

PLATE 7. *Yoseue* (Collective planting). Several trees are planted in one vessel in such a manner that they create the appearance of a wood or forest. (Japanese grey-bark elm. Age 50 years.)

PLATE 8. *Kengai* (Drooping trunk). This is an interesting type of tree often found in wild mountainous country or cliffs, exposed to all the severities of nature. It has a sense of profundity, but the disadvantage with this type of bonsai is that it lacks stability, and therefore it is very difficult to find a place in which it can be properly displayed. (Japanese black pine. Age 200 years.)

PLATE 9. *Ishizuki* (Tree with stone), (1) The trunk is planted in a shallow vessel in such a manner that it is embracing a rock. (Trident maple. Age about 80 years.)

PLATE 10. *Ishizuki* (Tree with stone), (2) This is another variety of *ishizuki*, in which the plant is set in a dant in the stone which is placed in a basin instead of an ordinary bonsai vessel. This type expresses a tree growing on top of a rocky cliff or an isolated island. (Five needle pine)

PLATE 11. Common Ezo spruce planted on a rock. 15 inches high and about 15 years old, it has been trained for 5 years.

PLATE 12. Beech. A plant taken from the mountains and planted as it would be in a grove as an ornament. Age 6 to 7 years. Height 11 inches.

PLATE 13. A flowering quince with small red flowers. Raised from a sprout cutting. Age 4 to 5 years. Height 1 foot.

PLATE 14. *Suiseki* (1) The art of *suiseki* is also embraced and loved by bonsai horticulturalists, although no plants are used, only stones or rocks. Natural stones and rocks with markings symbolizing mountains and gorges, or those which have patterns similar to flower petals are highly valued. This is a Kikka Stone symbolizing chrysanthemums.

PLATE 15. *Suiseki* (2) Tamba Stone. This stone suggests the scenery of an isolated island. Put it into a low flower basin for best effect.

PLATE 16. *Suiseki* (3) Kamo River Stone. This natural stone looks very much like a range of mountains, and gives the feeling of looking down from an airplane.

Plate 1.

Plate 2.

Plate 3.

Plate 4.

Plate 5.

Plate 7.

Plate 6.

Plate 8.

Plate 9.

Plate 10.

Plate 11.

Plate 13.

Plate 12.

Plate 14.

Plate 15.

Plate 16.

1. How to raise bonsai

NATURALLY, it is delightful to observe and appreciate a well-trained bonsai. However, I believe that there is greater pleasure in creating a bonsai for oneself. The pleasure of creation, of artistically raising an insipid plant growing in the mountains or fields into a dwarf tree—this is the first step in this hobby, and also where its real charm lies.

It is also something that can be enjoyed by anyone once he has gained some knowledge of the art of bonsai. Needless to say, it would be difficult for beginners to raise a top-flight bonsai, but, on the other hand, it is comparatively easy to create a dwarf tree of sufficient dignity to merit appreciation. I recommend readers to take up the art of raising bonsai for I believe that besides being a healthful occupation, it helps you develop a liking of and an intimacy with nature.

There are various methods of raising bonsai, and roughly divided they fall into the following categories:

1. Raising from a plant collected from a natural environment, or *yamadori*.
2. Raising by layering, or *toriki*.
3. Raising by separation of roots, or *kabuwake*.
4. Raising by planting a cutting, or *sashiki*.
5. Raising by grafting, or *tsugiki*.

6. Raising by seedage, or *misho*.
7. Raising from a seedling bought at a nursery.

I shall explain to readers the practical methods of raising bonsai according to the order listed. However, in this volume I will deal mainly with *coniferae* (especially evergreen needle-leaf trees) as this book is principally written for beginners and *coniferae* are best suited for this purpose as they are rigourous plants and easily raised.

1. RAISING FROM A PLANT COLLECTED FROM NATURAL ENVIRONMENT

When you are out on a hike or mountaineering, you come into contact with numerous and exquisite types of grasses and trees. Blessed by Mother Nature, they grow in countless shapes and forms, blossom forth with a colorful variety of flowers and bear fruit. If you could but unearth one of these, take it back home with you and place it in a pot where you would be able to gaze on its beauty, would it not be delightful? However, by no means will such a transferred plant always take root. Therefore the trick is in how to make certain that it will take root.

This method, known as *yamadori* (raising a bonsai from a plant collected in its natural environment), is the handiest way of raising a bonsai. All you have to do is find a plant that you consider suitable for a bonsai, and take it home. This can be done by anybody.

Most famous bonsai trees in Japan have been raised by the *yamadori* method, especially many Japanese black pine, Japanese red pine, Five needle pine, Needle juniper and Sargent juniper bonsai. Why is this so? If you raise a bonsai by seedage, it will take at least five to ten years just to shape the plant into an attractive bonsai. Furthermore, the toil and effort one must expend during the raising period is more than most bonsai lover are willing or able to afford. In addition, it is very difficult to create the appearance of age of the trunk, a special point regarding conifers. On the other hand, if you use the *yamadori* method, you will be able to utilize the shape of the tree already formed naturally, thereby greatly reducing the time required to train the plant so as to produce a bonsai worthy of appreciation.

Trees suitable for bonsai plants are available the world over, except in the frigid zones and a part of the tropical zones. So you do not have to be in Japan if you wish to raise a bonsai. Plants collected as material for bonsai are known as *araki* by Japanese bonsai horticulturists. And they raise these *araki* into bonsai.

The next question is in regard to the type of tree that one should select. There are so many species of trees to be found in the mountains and plains that their number may be counted in the thousands. But not all are fit to be used as material for bonsai. Some are totally unfit for this purpose, even though you expend great care and effort in bringing them home. There are others which can be created into bonsai but which will not grow well or amount to much of a bonsai. In other words, when you adopt the *yamadori* method, you have to select a plant that can easily be trained into becoming a bonsai and which is likely to grow into a plant that can be greatly appreciated.

Although most *coniferae* are qualified to be used for the creation of a bonsai, I will outline the major qualifications a plant should have.

1. The over-all shape of the plant should be such that it is small enough to be planted in a pot. Remember that the bonsai is a far cry from the normal trees that grow in one's garden. The bonsai, or potted dwarf tree, is trained to be minutely perfect so as to afford viewers an association with the grandness of nature in general and also permit them to admire its stately beauty. A small but compact shape is required.

2. The plant must have strong roots.

3. The tree must have comparatively small leaves which should be fairly thickly distributed.

4. It must have an interesting distribution of its branches and an attractive over-all appearance.

5. The plant should have enough vitality to ensure that it requires no special protective measures.

6. It should not be too tall, but rather have a natural dwarf-like stature, and yet have a lively vital force.

7. It should be of such a nature that it can be appreciated throughout the year, and furthermore, must have a comparatively long life span.

Although it is difficult to find an *araki* (material plant) meeting all these requirements, a small plant with much potential vitality and an interesting appearance is satisfactory. Other requirements for the ideal plant are a thick trunk with rough-looking bark and one that has densely growing leaves.

The Proper Season for Collecting "Araki"

Although there are slight seasonal differences in regard to the plants that you may choose, the best time is considered to be immediately before spring sprouting time. This also is the time when there is an improvement in the climate and the plants are easier to unearth.

It also is a time when the plant's roots can most easily *take* again after being replanted in a pot. At this time of the year, the plants have not as yet developed new roots, and those it has are not too lively, thereby reducing the chances of ruining the plant during the transplantation process.

In warm regions, that period from the latter part of February to the middle of March, and in the cool highland areas that period covering April and May are considered most suitable for the *yamadori* method.

The period considered a best second choice is that immediately before the plants enter the dormant season.

FIGURE 1. *The "yamadori" method of unearthing a plant. Unearth it as if you were simply pulling it right out of a bonsai vessel.*

How to Unearth a Plant

First decide upon the plant you wish to unearth and then out or remove all the grasses growing around it. Next carefully study the over-all shape of the tree and cut or trim those branches which you consider as unnecessary or too long, thereby facilitating the next step—digging.

Please note that you NEVER remove the plant by grasping it tightly in your hands and removing it forcibly. In so doing, you will ruin the trunk, tear the roots, scrape off the soil surrounding the ciliary roots, and probably render the plant unable to strike its roots when transplanted.

If the trunk of the tree you have selected has a diameter of 2 inches at its base, you draw a circle with a diameter of 4 to 6 inches around the plant. The tree and the surrounding soil within this circle must be unearthed together. Please note however that this is just a matter of principle. In fact, some trees spread long roots deep in the ground and

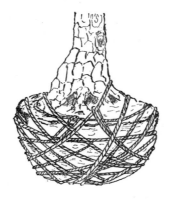

FIGURE 2. *How to wrap an uprooted tree—the roots and surrounding soil are wrapped in newspaper or straw mat, tied into place with string or straw rope.*

the area of soil which must be removed has to be enlarged accordingly.

In order to remove the plant, first dig a trough along the circle that you have traced around the plant. If you encounter any roots while digging this trough, cut them off with either a hoe or a pair of shears. You proceed in this manner, digging downwards and cutting the roots which spread out horizontally. When you have reached a depth approximately one-third the height of the plant, you beginning digging in toward the bottom of the tree you plan to remove, and under the soil which you intend to remove with the plant. If, while doing this, you encounter roots, cut them off in the aforementioned manner. Then cut the taproot spreading deep into the ground with a saw, and finally dig out the tree together with the surrounding soil (*Fig. 1*).

When you have completed removing the plant and soil, study it again and cut or trim those branches which you consider unnecessary. If the tree has new sprouts, pluck them off at their base. Also trim off those roots which emerge from the pot-shaped soil still surrounding the plant.

Next spray the soil with water from your canteen to moisten it,

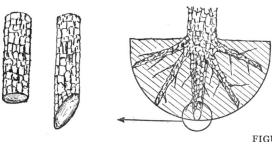

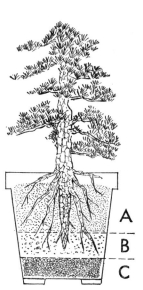

FIGURE 3. *Cut the roots diagonally.*

FIGURE 4. *Pot soil.* (A) *Fine grains of soil;* (B) *Larger grains than* A; (C) *" Goro-tsuchi."*

surround it with sphagna, and then wrap it in straw or newspapers, tying them into place with string or straw to facilitate carrying (*Fig. 2*).

Please note three important points : DO NOT crush the soil around the roots, DO NOT expose the tree to strong winds and DO NOT let the plant go dry.

How to Help the Tree Take Root

The *araki*, or bonsai material collected in the wilderness, must be transported in such a manner that it is not exposed directly to bright sunshine or strong winds, and with as few bumps and shakes as possible.

When you reach home, untie the string or rope binding your *araki* and carefully remove the wrapping you have used. It is best to leave the soil surrounding the roots untouched. Next trim the taproot, shortening it with a sharp blade in such a manner as to cut the end obliquely (*Fig. 3*). This protects the tree from water seeping in through the cut end and causing the tree to rot.

After being thus treated, the plant may be replanted temporarily in a field. However, since it is likely to be left unattended in such a case, it is advisable to plant it in a wooden tray or an unglazed pot. A hard porcelain pot is not fit for this purpose.

First, in order to facilitate drainage, fairly large grains of clean earth (approximately $\frac{1}{4}$ to $\frac{3}{8}$ inch in diameter) to make the first layer in the container. The second layer should consist of earth whose grains are a little smaller (perhaps mixed with little shingles). The root stock of the tree is placed on this foundation and clean, fine-grained earth preferably mixed with shingles is filled in around the roots (*Fig. 4*). Use a chopstick or something similar to thrust in around the roots so that the earth is tightly packed around them.

The tree should be planted in such a manner that it is steady and firm and stays put, while the root of the trunk should not be buried too deep.

Please try and avoid earth containing an over-abundance of fertilizer elements or which may contain harmful insects or bacteria.

I should have mentioned earlier that the container in which the plant is placed should have a small hole in its bottom. When you have completed the planting process, spray the tree from a watering can with relatively small nozzels until water begins to ooze out of the hole in the bottom of the container.

The transplanted tree is then kept in shade with the aid a reed screen for about twenty days so that sunshine reaches only the roots of the tree while the wind is kept off. Do not neglect to water the plant, especially to the extent where the surface of the earth may dry to the point where it turns whitish. The leaves also should be sprinkled with water once in a while. This sprinkling is known as *hamizu* in bonsai terminology.

The rules therefore are these: you must provide a proper amount of water, never letting the earth surrounding the plant dry up; do not expose it to the wind, and let only the base of the tree be exposed to the sunshine. Soon new sprouts will begin to grow, a sure sign that the tree is taking root. Normally it takes between twenty and thirty days for a tree to strike its roots after being transplanted, although this does vary with the type of tree. Needless to say, the younger trees strike roots faster than the older trees, and easier at that.

Steps to Be Taken After the Tree Strikes Roots

When the tree has struck its roots satisfactorily, new sprouts begin to grow and leaves unfold. This signals the time for you to remove the reed screen and allow the plant a little sunbathing. During the early stages of this process, the plant should be placed in the sunlight only in the mornings. Then later the sunbathing period can gradually be lengthened.

Fertilizer should not be used until after the tree has taken firm root, but once this has been accomplished, a little fertilizer will be satisfactory.

The new sprouts, if left unattended, usually grow to a larger size that they would have in a natural environment. This not only results in marring the over-all appearance of the tree but also checks the growth of the branches which are such a vital part of bonsai. (In principle, a good bonsai should have a dense distribution of branches.)

When the new sprouts have reached a length of about 1 inch, nip them off at their base with your finger nails. Healthy and strong new sprouts should be removed as close to their base as possible. However, the exact reverse is true for those which are growing badly. These should either be left untrimmed altogether or trimmed with the major portion being left.

About two to three weeks later, one to three new buds will emerge near the old sprout that had been trimmed. These new sprouts never grow to any length, while the short branches will now begin to show an improvement.

Trees which show little vitality, and whose trunks do not achieve a certain stoutness, are usually left untouched, their sprouts untrimmed, until they do show a certain healthy fitness.

As autumn draws to its close and winter nears, precautions must be taken to protect the tree from the cold and also from drying up. The tree, together with its container, is buried in well-drained ground exposed to plenty of sunlight. Sufficient earth should be packed around the roots and base of the tree, and this should in turn be covered with straw. I do not believe that anything need be said about careful watering of this tree during the winter season.

The tree is again transplanted in either March or April after the winter season is over. This time a real bonsai pot, or *honbachi*, is used to add to the appreciation of the tree. The manner in which this transplanting is done, and the care which follows, will be explained later in this volume.

You should know at this point, however, that it usually takes two to three years for a plant collected in the wilds to be developed into a bonsai of appreciable quality.

2. Raising by Layering, or " Toriki "

Raising a bonsai by layering may be the second easiest method. When you find a branch which you consider as having the proper qualities to be developed into a fine bonsai, first let it develop roots. Then remove it from the trunk of the tree and transplant it in a pot. With this method, it is possible not only to choose material with an ideal shape but also to develop it into a bonsai in a comparatively short time.

However, this layering method cannot be utilized in regard to trees which do not develop roots from its trunk or branches. Therefore your choice is limited to certain trees such as the Pomegranate, Crape-myrtle,

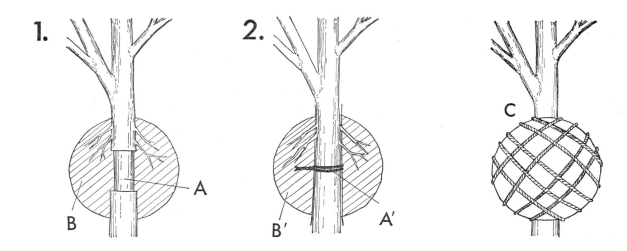

FIGURE 5. *Tow layering methods. 1. (A) Remove bark and inner fibrous bark. (B) Wrap sphagna around the area. 2. (A') Tightly bind with wire. (B') Wrap sphagna around the area. (C) Cover the whole with a sheet of vinyl or a straw mat and secure with string.*

English holly, Maple, Elm, and Cryptomeria. Some *coniferae* such as Common Ezo spruce often can be used successfully also. Pine is difficult to raise by the layering method, but it is possible if you are prepared to handle them with great patience for a period of two to three years.

Best Season for Layering

In Japan, the best time of the year is during May and June. In other words, that time of year when temperatures are fairly high, as is the humidity. If you miss this period, the branch being layered won't strike its roots in the following autumn, and you have to wait until the next spring or autumn.   In addition, the plant needs great care in the winter, being properly watered while that part of it below ground must not be allowed to become frozen.   Layering during the months of March and April is possible.

Steps in Layering

First choose a branch you think has the proper appearance for a bonsai tree.   Next select that portion of the branch where you wish it to *take root* and, using a sharp blade, peel the bark of that part to a width of $\frac{3}{4}$ to $1\frac{1}{4}$ inches.   Now tightly wrap this *naked* part of the branch with sphagna which has been dipped in water and formed into a ball shape. The sphagna should be at least three times as thick as the branch it is wrapped around, and fastened into place with a strong rope (*Fig. 5–1*).

Another method is to tightly bind that part of the branch you have chosen to unpeel with copper wire, and then wrap the sphagna around it.   In this manner, the same affect is achieved as the wire cuts into the bark as the branch grows (*Fig. 5–2*).   Good results usually are achieved when this method is applied to trees which have a smooth bark and whose trunk and branches have a fast rate of growth.

Wrapping the branch with sphagna and fastening it into place with a strong straw rope is just as well for your purpose, however, also wrap the sphagna with a sheet of plastic which has a funnel-shaped upper end to allow an easy water absorption, and to protect it from drying out, and occasionally dampen it down.

If your attempt is a failure, your *tree* will wither and die within one or two weeks.   Otherwise, the plant will strike roots by early autumn.

When the branch has sprouted sufficient roots, it should be sawed off at a point beneath the ball of sphagna and transplanted in a container or vessel.   However, the utmost caution should be exercised not to saw the branch off too early as the roots may be endangered.   Some of the sphagna should be left attached to the branch to protect the roots from possible damage.

When the branch is removed from the tree, it is advisable not to do so in one fell swoop. First saw halfway through the branch and then leave it for about one week, after which you can complete the removal if you think that all is well. The chances of failure are greatly reduced when such caution is exercised.

After the branch has been transplanted in a pot, it should be supported by a prop to keep the roots immobile, and excessive branches should be trimmed off in order to reduce evaporation of the plant's moisture. Sudden exposure to sunlight is harmful and very *weak* fertilizers should be used to begin with.

The following spring the tree must again be transplanted, this time to a *honbachi* or bonsai vessel which adds to the appreciative qualities of the bonsai, much as a frame does for a painting.

When transplanting the tree, check the roots carefully and remove the remaining sphagna. Also remove that lower part of the trunk where no roots are growing.

Interesting advantages of the layering method are as follows :

1) A small tree which is too tall to be a good bonsai can be raised into two bonsai trees, as can one having too long a branch. In the latter case the original trunk and one of the branches being used as independent bonsai.

2) A tree which looks ugly because of withered lower branches can be made into a shorter bonsai by utilizing the upper, and better looking, portion of its trunk.

3) A tree which has a poor over-all appearance can be raised into an excellent bonsai if it has one superb branch.

4) Several, and sometimes scores, of *araki*, or bonsai materials, can be obtained from a single mother tree.

5) *Araki* may be taken from old as well as young trees, and yet it will seldom affect the former to the extent that it will cause it to die.

6) A bonsai can be raised in a comparatively short period of time by this method.

3. Raising by Separation of Roots, or " Kabuwake "

This method is unfit for *coniferae*, but I shall still describe it as a matter of reference.

Shrubs and perennial plants can easily be propagated by means of separation of the roots. Suitable species are the Wax tree, Mulberry tree, White birch, Quince, Magnolia, Gardenia, Rhododendron, Azalea, Silverberry and Akebia.

Plants which have been *multiplied* by the separation of their roots have exactly the same characteristics as the mother plant. They also grow much faster, and yield more flowers and seeds than those propagated by seedage.

When shrubs are *multiplied* through separation of the roots, each of the separated plants has already begun to develop its own characteristics. Therefore, they are easier to train into good bonsai in a comparatively short period of time and with relatively little care.

Best Season and Method

In general, it is best to carry out the separation in the springtime just before sprouts appear. If the separation is conducted during this time of the year, most kinds of plants can be successfully propagated.

In the case of perennial plants, just dig them up and divide them with a pair of horticultural shears into a number of adequately-sized plants. Tear off all withered leaves and remove rotten roots, and then plant them in pots or vessels. It is as simple as that.

Where shrubs are concerned, choose one that has a good distribution of branches, and then dig around it with a hoe. Sever the root with a saw at that place where the mother plant is connected with its *child* plants. Remember to take care that you do not ruin of the ciliary roots when you unearth the plant. Also discard all unnecessary branches and leaves.

When you have unearthed the plant, trim the main root with a sharp knife, making an oblique cut that will point directly downwards. Carefully shake off the soil still clinging to the roots ; remove any unnecessary branches and leaves that still are left in order to train the plant into roughly the shape you desire, and then plant the plant in either a wooden tray or an unglazed pot. The method used here is the same as that of the *yamadori* method. Do not plant it too deep.

Once you have done this, be sure to provide it with plenty of water and keep it under a reed screen for about twenty days, thereby protecting it from strong breezes and allowing sunlight to reach only the base of the plant. Water the plant carefully so that the earth surrounding it never gets dry or whitish in color, and also sprinkle water over the leaves occasionally.

For detailed instructions, please refer to the chapter dealing with the *yamadori* method.

4. RAISING BY PLANTING A CUTTING, OR " SASHIKI "

When the branches of a young tree collected in the wilderness, in connection with the *yamadori* method, begin to grow, you are offered another source of horticultural pleasure. You can make a cutting from these branches and plant it, for, while training the tree, you must remove all unnecessary branches to bring about the well-balanced shape that you require. And these discarded branches can themselves be used.

Naturally, this is not the reason the cutting method is used in bonsai. It is employed because some trees strike roots easily and quickly develop from a cutting.

Adopting this method enables you to obtain material for several bonsai at one time. Furthermore, they inherit the same characteristics as their *mother* tree. An excellent mother tree will supply you with many good *araki*. However, one of the disadvantages of this cutting method is that it takes many years to train the cutting into a fair bonsai.

The best species among those plants suitable for the cutting method are the Elm, Cryptomeria and Azalea. The next best are the Common Ezo spruce, Camellia, Maple and Quince. The Five needle pine and Apricot are considered a little too difficult to raise by this method.

In short, the cutting method is a system of propagation in which you remove part of a plant and then transplant it so it may take root for the express purpose of providing you with the material for a bonsai.

This method is divided into four categories: (1) *ha-zashi*, or leaf cutting; (2) *shinme-zashi*, or sprout cutting; (3) *eda-zashi*, or branch cutting; and (4) *ne-zashi*, or root cutting. However, since the major plants considered for bonsai in this volume are of the *coniferae* species, only the second and third categories will be explained. Needless to say, the most popular category is that of *eda-zashi*, branch cutting.

A branch which is to be planted is known technically as *sashi-ho* (cutting).

Best Season to Plant Cuttings

Although this varies with the type of tree and the method employed, the latter two-thirds part of March is most suitable where Tokyo is concerned, and one or two months later where colder regions are concerned. The plainest way to explain this is to say that the best time is that time when the new sprouts have yielded leaves and branches.

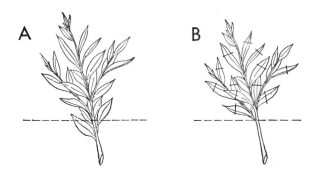

A   B

FIGURE 6. *How to make a scion. Remove all leaves on the lower third of the scion* (A–B), *and trim upper leaves* (B).

FIGURE 7. *How to plant cuttings. A ball of red clay around the roots of the cutting facilitates root-taking. The ball of clay should be 3/4 to 1-1/4 inch in diameter.*

How to Choose and Obtain " Sashi-ho " or Cuttings

Generally, young and soft cuttings are superior to those older and harder as they have more vitality necessary to striking roots and growing stronger. Let us first take up the *shinme-zashi*, or sprout cutting method. A newly grown sprout is cut diagonally with a sharp blade. Remove all leaves on the lower one-third of the branch, and two-thirds of the leaves on the other part of the branch should be trimmed to one-third their length in order to help decrease the evaporation of moisture in the branch to a minimum (*Fig. 6*).

RAISING BY PLANTING A CUTTING, OR " SASHIKI " • 41

In the *eda-zashi*, or branch cutting method, a branch one or three years old, healthy and unharmed by insects should be selected.

The cutting should be anywhere from 1¼ inches to 6 inches in length. It is best to keep the cutting in a water-filled container of fairly large size so that it will not lose its moisture. Often the nether end of the cutting is wrapped in a ball of clean clayish soil ¾ to 1¼ inches in diameter and then planted in earth (*Fig. 7*).

How to Prepare a Bed for the Cutting

Soil in which the cutting is to be planted should be clean and able to retain moisture, be well drained and contain little fertilizer. A mixture of seven parts red loam to three parts of sand is commonly used.

You may use either a pot or a wooden tray, but they should not be too deep. Vessels 4 to 6 inches deep are ideal. Use large-grained soil which drains well for the first layer in the container, and then fill it up with the fine-grained soil to a point a little below the lip. Next level the surface of the soil by pressing it lightly with your hands.

How to Plant a Cutting

Leaving a proper distance between each cutting (if you transplant more than one in the same container), plant them in an inclined position so that one-third of the total length of the cutting is buried (*Fig. 8*). Do not thrust them directly into the ground as this may result in scraping the bark where it has been cut and so reduce its chances of striking roots.

Instead, form a small hole in the soil with your finger and then insert the cutting, carefully and gently pressing soil around the base. Use a pair of tweezers to hold the cuttings if they are thin or short in length.

Aftercare

Using a watering can with very small openings in its rose, sprinkle

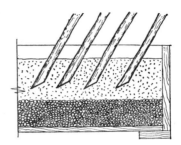

FIGURE 8. *How to plant cuttings. Leaving ample room between each cutting, insert them with a slight inclination so that one-third of their length is buried.*

sufficient water over the cuttings. Until they have struck their roots, keep them under a reed screen to protect them from the wind and avoid direct rays of the sun. At night, remove the screen so that they are moistened by the night dew.

During the first month, sprinkle water on the leaves about three or four times a day. Such sprinkling must be done in such a way that the surface of the soil does not show an excess of water.

The cuttings will strike their roots about a month after being transplanted, and will begin to sprout. When this occurs, you begin to expose them to the sun, gradually extending the length of time of the exposure. Also the frequency of *hamizu* should be reduced to just twice a day. Water the plant as you would an ordinary bonsai once in the morning and once in the evening; however, if the surface of the ground is too dry, it is good to water it once in the afternoon. Use a weak fertilizer.

During the winter, they should be placed in a warm place where there is no breeze. Sprinkle water occasionally to keep the earth moistened properly. By the time the spring has come your way again, the cuttings will have struck strong roots and developed little branches.

5. RAISING BY GRAFTING, OR "TSUGIKI"

Grafting is a method of propagation in which part of a plant or sprout is removed and then, as a rule, tightly joined to a tree of the same species in order to raise a new *araki*, or bonsai material. The rootstock is known as *daiki* and the scion as *tsugi-ho*.

An advantage of this grafting method is that the *araki* so raised inherits the qualities of the scion. Also, if you have scions of good quality, it is possible to raise as many *araki* as you wish. It does, however, have its disadvantages. It requires a fair degree of skill and, no matter how well it is done, the graft often leaves a scar on the tree which mars its appearance. In addition, the stions (scion and rootstock) appear to have a shorter life span than those independent trees which have been propagated by means of the seedage method or collected in the wilderness.

And yet, grafting is a very convenient method of raising material for bonsai as all you need is a good scion. This is especially true when you are unable to obtain *araki* by other means.

Grafting Methods

Of the several grafting methods, such as branch grafting, sprout grafting and root grafting, the most popular in Japan is that of branch grafting. In particular, this is the only method used when raising bonsai material from *coniferae*. Therefore, in this volume, I shall deal with this method alone. Branch grafting is classified as *ten-tsugi* or *moto-tsugi* according to the placement of the graft.

Best Season for Grafting

The best season for grafting in Tokyo is considered to be that period from the middle of February to the middle of March. In warmer regions grafting would take place before this time of the year, while in colder regions it would be done later.

Rootstock Preparation

A rootstock should be young and healthy, and equipped with many roots. Seedlings two to three years old are most popular. They are either raised by seedage or collected from a natural environment, and are trained to meet the requirements of a rootstock.

How to Make Scions

It is of the utmost importance that scions be obtained from trees with a good heritage as they will form the very trunk of the bonsai. The qualifications of the donor tree are that its leaves must be short and densely distributed. If the tree is of the needle-leaf species, the leaves should be beautifully straight and lacking in twists or bends.

When the donor tree has been selected, remove one of the small but strong branches that had sprouted in the spring of the previous year. The branch must be severed as close to the trunk of the tree as possible. The severed end of this scion is then placed in shaded wet sand to protect it from withering while you prepare for the actual graft.

Points of Grafting

First, it is best to carry out the grafting process on a fine, windless day. I shall now explain the *ten-tsugi*, or top grafting, process. Prepare a scion of approximately $1\frac{1}{4}$ inches in length. Using a sharp knife, cut off the branch of the tree you have chosen for your rootstock in such manner that it still has a few lower leaves. Then pierce the cut end vertically with the blade of your knife to a depth of half an inch.

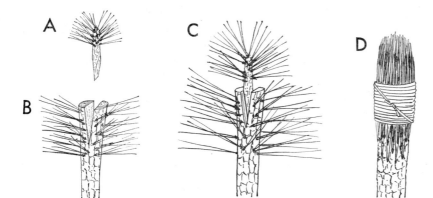

FIGURE 9. *How to make "tentsugi".*
Shape end of scion into wedge (A).
Cut slit in stock (B). *Insert wedge end*
of scion into stock's slit (C). *Then*
(D) *tie stions together.*

Next remove the lower leaves of the scion and whittle its end into a wedge form which you tightly squeeze into the incision made in the rootstock (*Fig. 9*).

Let us now take up the *moto-tsugi*, or bottom grafting, process. First cut the end of the scion diagonally with a knife. Make a similar cut on the other side to obtain the shape as illustrated in Figure 10, Position A, B. The surface length of the cut should be shorter than a length equal to two or three times the diameter of the scion's trunk.

Next make a diagonal slit as close to the base of the rootstock as is possible. The depth of the slit should be equal to one-third the diameter of the rootstock, and the same size as the cut end of the scion. Then insert the scion firmly in the slit. Use a piece of raffia or straw to keep the graft firmly in place (*Fig 10*).

Earth in which the rootstock is to be planted should be clean, free

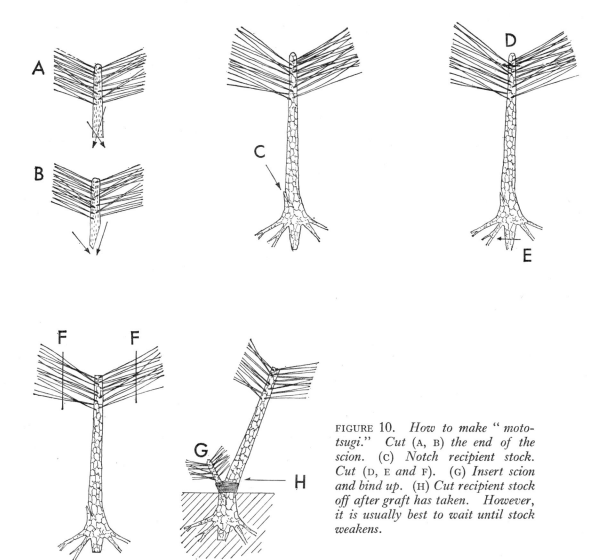

FIGURE 10. *How to make " moto-tsugi." Cut (A, B) the end of the scion. (C) Notch recipient stock. Cut (D, E and F). (G) Insert scion and bind up. (H) Cut recipient stock off after graft has taken. However, it is usually best to wait until stock weakens.*

RAISING BY GRAFTING, OR " TSUGIKI " • 47

of insects and containing little fertilizer, and should be able to drain well. The major root of the rootstock should be removed before it is transplanted, and leaves should be trimmed to half-size (*Fig. 10*). This is to restrain natural growth of the rootstock and thereby facilitating an easy merger of the scion and stock. A wooden tray or unglazed pot may be used in which to transplant the rootstock.

Aftercare

When the grafting process is completed, keep the stion, as the combined scion-rootstock is called, in a shady place protected from the wind. Expose it to the sun gradually. Keep the earth properly moist, avoiding excessive watering as this may cause a rotting effect in the roots.

If the graft is a success, the leaves of the scion should show vitality and begin to sprout about a month later. The straw or raffia wrapping may now be removed and a weak solution of fertilizer used. If you have utilized the *ten-tsugi* method, you should keep adding fertilizer for a period of two to three years so that the trunk will grow thick and stout.

Transplanting of the tree to a bonsai pot should be carried out either in the spring or autumn, at which time you should cut the taproot short to spurt the growth of smaller roots.

In the event you have used the *moto-tsugi* method, wait until the scion has regained strength after the graft. Then remove the leaves on the upper part of the rootstock to prevent the stock from growing unnecessarily. Remove the upper portion of the rootstock in the spring or autumn of the following year when it weakens. If the stion has grown strong enough, it can now be transplanted to a bonsai pot.

It takes two to five years for the grafted plant to be transformed into an appreciable bonsai.

Layering method (1)

PLATE 17. *The "toriki", or layering method, applied to a Common Ezo spruce at two places: one on horizontal branch at left and another at center on trunk.*

PLATE 18. *Bonsai raised by the layering method with a supporting stick.*

49

Layering method (2)

Grafting method

PLATE 21. *Five needle pine seedlings obtained by the " mototsugi " method, or bottom grafting method, are raised in wooden trays.*

PLATE 22. *Pines raising by seedage. (From left to right) Ten years (about 9 inches high), five years, and two years old.*

PLATE 23. *Seedlings, about 13 months after sowing.*

PLATE 24. *Five needle pine seedlings being raised in field. They also may be raised in vessels, but the field method provides the seedlings with vitality in a comparatively short period of time.*

Vessels

PLATES 25–33. *Vessels of various shapes.*

26. *" Maru-bachi "*, *or circular vessel.*

25. *" Choho-bachi "*, *or rectangular vessel.*

27. *" Koban-bachi "*, *or oval vessel.*

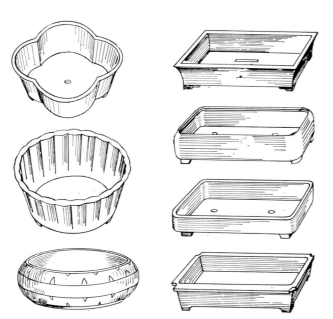

FIGURES 11–17. *Vessels of various shapes.*
(From top of the left) " *Mokko* ", " *Wabana* ",
" *Taikodo* ", *(Right)* " *Sotoen* ", " *Uchien* ",
" *Nadekaku* ", " *Sumiire* ".

28. " *Masugata-bachi* ", or square vessel.

29. " *Rokkaku-bachi* ", or hexagonal vessel.

30. " *Fukuroshiki-bachi* ", or vessel with lip projecting inwards.

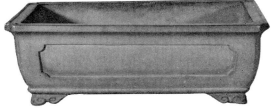

31. " *Gakuiri* ". So-called because the side of the vessels looks like a picture frame.

32. " *Dohimo* ". So-called because the vessel has a string-like belt around its outside walls.

33. " *Kumoashi* ", or legs with cloud pattern.

53

Transcripting

1

PLATES 34–36. 1) *Remove unnecessary leaves and branches.* 2) *Loosen soil with bamboo sticks.* 3) *Dig the tree out carefully. Try not to grab the trunk.*

4

5

2

3

PLATES 37–40. 4) *Place the up-rooted bonsai on the table.* 5) *Loosen soil around the roots with a bamboo stick.* 6) *Cut root hair after removing the soil.* 7) *Trim short all ciliary roots. When the tap root is too big to fit into the vessel, shorten it with a diagonal cut.*

6

7

55

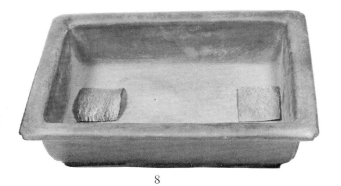

8

9

PLATES 45–47. 12) *Probe with bamboo stick to ensure firm packing.* 13) *Fine grains of soil are spread on the surface and evened out with a trowel.* 14) *Sprinkle water carefully after the transplantation.*

12

PLATES 41–44. 8) *Drainage holes covered with barks of hemp palm. The bark may be replaced by a double layer of thin net made from vinyl.* 9) *Sift the soil to obtain the grains in the various required sizes. Start with the large 3/8 inch mesh and then use the smaller size meshes in turn.* 10) *Place the soil in the vessel.* 11) *Set the plant in the vessel.*

10

11

13

14

Leaf-cutting

PLATES 48, 49. *Leaf-cutting, or "hagari." Leave 1/4 inch of leaf stalk at the base. Below is a Maple bonsai leaves of which have been only half cut.*

Wiring

PLATE 50. *Points of wiring. First anchor the wire on a branch growing vertically and then start applying the wire to the branches or trunk where you wish to make some corrections in shape. Bind the wire fairly tightly and you will be guaranteed of making an effective correction. Hold the branch firmly with one hand.*

PLATES 51–54. *Process of bonsai training.* 1) *This Maple has excessively grown branches after new spring sprouts have grown.* 2) *Remove all the leaves, leaving a small portion of the leaf stalk.* 3) *Those branches which have grown too long or may spoil the over-all appearance of the bonsai should be removed.* 4) *Wire the plant into the over-all shape that you require. Upon completion of all these steps, the plant can finally be called a bonsai.*

Training (2)

PLATES 55–57. *The practice of " sei-shi ". (1) Seven-year-old Five needle pine propagated by " misho ", or seedage, as it looks before " seishi ". 2) Remove unnecessary branches. Then making your mind up as to the shape you desire, wire the tree into said shape. 3) After wiring, the tree has gained a nice shape featuring a " shakan ", or leaning trunk.*

Shelf and stall

PLATE 58. *Bonsai shelves.*

PLATE 59. *Bonsai stall.*

61

PLATE 60. *Bonsai display.*

PLATE 61. *Display of "ishizuki" bonsai.*

6. Raising by Seedage, or "Misho"

The *misho* method, or raising by seedage, is another means of obtaining material for a bonsai. However, this is a process that requires several years to complete, and, in addition, there is a problem in obtaining seeds. Therefore, I shall omit this process from this volume.

7. Raising from a Seedling

Seedlings are quite easy to obtain as even city-dwellers can find them at nurseries in their neighborhood. Select one which is not too large but which has a stout root, strong trunk and well distributed branches. I'm sure that you will derive a great deal of pleasure just from making a tour of the nursery gardens in an effort to find the seedling of your choice. The best season for this process is the March-May period.

Ordinarily, seedlings are wrapped around their roots with earth or sphagna. When you arrive home with your prize, remove such wrapping as soon as possible and plant the seedling in an unglazed pot. Trim the roots if they are too long.

Aftercare

Aftercare in this case is the same as that used in the *yamadori* method. However, unlike the plants obtained in that method, the seedling has already acquired a certain strength, so that you may use fertilizer (in controlled quantities, naturally) a lot sooner.

2. Transplantation

TRANSPLANTATION is of the utmost importance regarding bonsai. The bonsai is planted in a shallow vessel which contains a minimum amount of soil required to keep the tree alive. Additionally, although the growth rate of dwarf trees may vary, they all develop numerous roots within a few years and absorb all the nutritious elements in the soil until such time as there is no further room in which new roots can develop. If the plant is left unattended, it will wither and die for lack of water.

Therefore, the transplantation of a bonsai is, so to speak, a form of rejuvenation without which the plant cannot live. A well-kept bonsai lasts for hundreds of years in its little pot.

Transplantation also gives you the opportunity of directly studying any damage that may have been wrought by decay in the roots or an invasion of bugs, and thereby take measures to repair such damage. Another advantage is that it gives you a chance to examine the stage of the soil and the roots, and see whether the soil is fit for the plant or there is sufficient fertilizer.

The frequency of transplantation depends on the type of tree and its age. *Coniferae*, which have a rather slow rate of growth, generally are transplanted every three to four years. On the other hand, broad-leafed trees develop their roots so fast that they fill a vessel within a year, and so must be transplanted with greater frequency.

Naturally, even where the same type of tree is concerned, the older trees grow at a slow rate and do not require much nourishment, while the livelier younger trees grow rapidly, filling the vessels with their roots, and consuming all the nutritious elements in the soil within a comparatively short time.

The tree will show signs of weakening when transplantation is overdue. If you observe carefully, you will notice that the color of the leaves fades, the lower leaves wither, branches will wither and sometimes the surface of the soil will swell out and harden because of overgrown roots. Once this occurs the soil has difficulty in absorbing sufficient water sprinkled on the plant over-flowing out over the lip of the vessel. The ventilation spaces in the soil become clogged with fine hairy roots which choke up the natural supply of air and moisture. If a plant is kept in this manner, even a masterpiece cannot maintain its high standard.

1. BEST SEASON FOR TRANSPLANTATION

As with everything else, the best time for transplanting a bonsai depends on the age and species of the tree, the type of tree and the local climate. Generally speaking, though, the best time of year for transplanting is in the spring when the trees begin sprouting. Narrowed down further, it is that period between the time the sap begins actively circulating until sprouting begins that is considered most appropriate. This period is really the ideal period of the year regarding transplantation as even those trees best transplanted at other times will not wither or weaken if transplanted at this time.

Since there is some difference, even among trees of the same species, in their sprouting time, those which are fast growers should be transplanted comparatively early in this season, and vice versa for the slow growers. Naturally, the local climate and weather conditions should be taken into consideration.

If you fail to carry out, for some unavoidable reason, the transplanting in the spring, the next best thing is to do so the following autumn, between the middle of September and the middle of October, at the latest. It should not be carried out any later as the winter cold may ruin the tree.

Certain species of trees do not have it in their nature to develop new roots after transplanting in the autumn, among them the Pomegranate, Citrus, Needle juniper and tropical trees. So please transplant your bonsai in the spring.

How often should bonsai be transplanted? As I have previously explained, *coniferae* (Pine, Common Ezo spruce, Cryptomeria, Needle juniper, Japanese yew, Hemlock spruce, Torreya, Hinoki cypress, etc.) should be transplanted once every two or three years if they are young and fast growers, and every five or six years for the older trees.

Apricot, Cherry, Peach, Quince, Aronia, Silk tree, Beech tree, Elm, Red-leafed hornbeam, Maple, and Wax tree grow roots so quickly that the bonsai vessel will be tightly packed within a year. Therefore, these species should be transplanted once every year.

2. BONSAI VESSELS

Bonsai vessels are divided into two groups, these being Japanese and Chinese makes. Aged Chinese vessels are highly valued among bonsai horticulturists. Perhaps because of the excellence in quality of the raw materials, Chinese vessels have a soft, smooth appearance, and yet are possessed of an adequately hard surface.

They have good drainage and ventilation, and at the same time maintain a satisfactory standard of moisture in the soil. In addition, their graceful appearance makes them more than fitting for the practical raising and proper appreciation of bonsai. Japanese bonsai lovers highly value the so-called *Kowatari* which were made more than two-hundred years ago. *Chuwatari* and *Shinwatari* are the generic terms given to two groups of bonsai vessels made in China. The *Shinwatari* are comparatively new ones which were made in China during the 1910s and 1920s on special order from Japan. However, those produced in Japan today are of equal quality as the Chinese items except that they lack that certain elegance possessed by the Chinese products that was engendered through centuries of history.

There are not many of the Chinese vessels available today, especially the *Kowatari*, and this rarity has boosted their price to a point where they are classified as artistic masterpieces.

Be that as it may, Japanese unglazed pots are quite sufficient for the purpose of raising bonsai and can create an equal air of appreciation. And yet nothing can surpass the Chinese *Kowatari*, if you consider them as objects of art in themselves.

Various Shapes of Vessels (See pages 52, 53)

Bonsai vessels are classified by their general shape, and also in relation to the shape of certain parts of the vessels. Under the first category comes such shapes as rectangular, circular, square, oval, *mokko*, *rinkashiki*, hexagonal, octagonal, *fukuroshiki*, and drum body shaped.

The second category takes into consideration the shapes of certain parts of the vessels, as follows, together with the names applied to these shapes :

Shape of vessel's brim : *uchien* and *sotoen*

Shape of vessel's corners : *naze-kaku* and *sumi-iri*.
Surface of the sides of the vessels : *gakuiri* (*gakumen*), *dohimo* and *jobuna*.
Shape of the vessel's legs : *kumoashi*.

How to Choose Bonsai Vessels

Unglazed earthenware pots are considered the best in regard to the cultivation of bonsai as they permit good drainage, at the same time serving to retain the warmth. A well-shaped and flawless old Chinese vessel may cost thousands of dollars, but contemporary Japanese products are quite sufficient in serving the purpose of training the bonsai. In this chapter I will explain how to select a vessel in regard to the shape and color of the pot.

A. Appropriateness of Vessels Regarding Shape

1. For a single straight tree or a dynamic leaning tree, a rather deep rectangular vessel is the answer. However, for those straight trees having a rather thin and stylish trunk, a square or multi-sided vessel is best.

2. A shallow oval vessel harmonizes with bonsai having two trunks.

3. For trees planted in groups (*yose-ue*) or a densely planted group of thin trunks such as *netsuranari*, a shallow circular, oval or *mokko* shape is recommended. Vessels with depth are not fit.

4. For the drooping type (*kengai*) of bonsai, a deep square pot is utilized.

5. *Ishi-zuki* (or roots growing out of and embracing a rock) is best matched with a very shallow rectangular vessel or *suiban* (a vessel which does not have a small drainage hole in its bottom).

B. Appropriateness of Vessels Regarding Color

1. Plain pots of subdued hue best fit the *coniferae*. (Red earthen-

ware, purple earthware, *udei* family of color.)   White or yellow vessels would be far to bright to harmonize with the plants.

2.   A vessel for flower plants must be selected according to the color of the flowers.   For instance, plants bearing whitish flowers, such as the Apricot and Quince would match well with light yellow or willow green vessels, while light or dark blue vessels would go well with reddish flowers, and dark green vessels with yellowish flowers.

3.   Maple, Wax tree, Ivy and Ginkgo usually harmonize with willow green or dark blue vessels.

4.   Aronia, English holly, Apple, Persimmon, etc., are best teamed up with rather plain and rustic purple earthenware which shows off their bright-colored fruits to good advantage.

Now we come to the relation between the size of the tree and that of the pot.   This may be looked at from two different viewpoints, one being the heighth of the tree and the other the span of the branches stretched out in all directions.

Placing emphasis on the height rather than the span of the tree, a suitable vessel would be one whose length is equal to about two-thirds the tree's height.   If the tree is 2 feet high, then a vessel 1 foot 4 inches long would be suitable.

On the other hand, if the trees specific feature is the distribution of its branches, a vessel measuring seven or eight-tenths the total span of the branches is suitable.   That is, if the total span of the branches measures 2 feet, then the vessel used should be approximately 1½ feet in length.

If you use a new unglazed earthen vessel, first submerge it in water for about 30 minutes so that it may absorb sufficient moisture.   This results in better care for the plant later on.

The drainage hole in the bottom of the pot must be carefully checked. If the hole has an elevated ridge, it is unsatisfactory as this results in poor drainage which in turn causes the roots to spoil. If the pot's hole has such a ridge, grind it down with an abrasive, or simply make another hole by its side to facilitate satisfactory drainage. Currently, bonsai horticulturalists are placing a double layer of thin net made from vinyl, or bark of hemp palm.

3. EARTH OR SOIL

In principle, the most suitable soil for a bonsai is that in which the tree had originally grown. However, it being practically impossible to collect soil in which the plant originally grew, bonsai enthusiasts select several kinds of so-called basic soil which they apply in certain combinations according to the type of plant involved. Generally speaking, bonsai, and plants in general, adapt themselves to the circumstances and the environment. Therefore, this inborn nature may be developed through cultivation.

In this chapter I will outline the different kinds of soil that are currently in use in Japan. Explanations will follow later on how to prepare bonsai soil from ordinary earth obtained in a particular locality. A few characteristics of bonsai soil must first be explained before proceeding further.

First, the soil should be clean and almost free of natural fertilizer. Nourishment must be fed the plant through artificial fertilizer. This is because differences in soil means different amounts of fertilizing elements, and this fact alone prohibits a stable and balanced raising of bonsai.

Secondly, bonsai soil is made up of numerous particles. When they are placed in the vessel, they create very tiny *rooms* which permit the proper flow and distribution of air and water, and at the same time store moisture for the plant.

Because of these tiny *rooms*, a bonsai can grow in a very small container. The smooth flow of water and air in the pot soil naturally facilitates a high rate of metabolism and the resultant favorable growth of the plant.

Basic Soil

Kuropoka : Typical soil of this type is found in the Musashino plateau in the western suburbs of greater Tokyo. But it can be found everywhere in the world. It is a soft, blackish and slightly viscous granular soil. It contains a fair amount of fertilizing elements, and has the ability to hold a good quantity of water, or moisture. It is sometimes used in raising Elm and Maple trees, but it is always mixed with other soil because it is unable to maintain its granular form for a long period of time and results in poor drainage. It usually constitutes the topsoil.

Kuro-tsuchi (Black loam) : This soil is found one layer lower than the aforementioned *kuropoka*. Containing less fertilizing elements than *kuropoka*, *kurotsuchi* is dark, soft and clean soil which sustains its granular form for a comparatively long period of time. This is therefore better suited for bonsais than *kuropoka*.

Aka-tsuchi (Red loam) : This soil has a reddish or brownish coloration. It maintains its granular form for quite a long period and also contains little fertilizing elements. It is very clean, and yet has good moisture-retention abilities, making it the best soil for use where bonsai are concerned. *Akatsuchi* can be found in various places the world over, but in Japan it is largely found in the Kanto plateau area. Many bonsai horticulturalists in Japan use this soil, mixed with a small amount of shingles, in raising bonsai trees of all types.

Arakida-tsuchi : This is soil found at the bottom of rice paddy field. And heavy and sticky dark grey soil, it is often used to make roof slates or in the building of mud walls. Although it does not permit good drainage, it contains few fertilizing elements, and has good qualities where the retention of moisture and the absorbing of fertilizer are concerned. It is regarded as best for such water plants as the Water lily and those which consume large quantities of water, such as the Willow.

Kanuma-tsuchi (Light clay and sand): This is a yellowish-brown soil found two layers down in the fields of the Kanuma and Utsunomiya area of the Kanto district in Japan. A light and soft soil, it contains a great deal of moisture, and yet has good drainage qualities because it maintains its granular form for long period. This soil is suitable for Azalea and Selaginella which require a lot of moisture.

Fuyodo (Leaf mold): A soft, light, darkish brown soil consisting mainly of decayed leaves and branches. Artifical leaf mold now is being sold at nurseries. It is usually mixed with other kinds of soil when employed in raising bonsai that features tree flowers and fruit.

Keto-tsuchi (Peat): A peaty, dark brownish and sticky soil consisting of water oats and reeds which have been buried and decayed. This is usually used when the bonsai is attached to a rock.

Tenjingawa-suna (River sand): A kind of sand usually found in river beds, consisting of hard grains that contain iron. It is the result of granite that has been weathered away by the natural elements. It is clean and permits good drainage, while its hard and rough surface forces the bonsai to extend many ciliary roots. This, together with *akatsuchi*, is a must for raising *coniferae*. This soil was so named because it is found in the Tenjin River in Hyogo Prefecture. Any good quality sand can be used as a substitute.

Mizugoke, or Sphagna: A type of moss found in damp areas, it is soft, has a braid shape and an average length of 5 to 7 inches. It is dried in the sun after being collected. Since sphagna contains little fertilizing elements and at the same time is capable of holding large amounts of moisture, it is used in connection with plants that require large amounts of water. It also is very useful when raising bonsai in the *yamadori* and *toriki* (layering) methods.

The Preparation of Bonsai Soil

The aforementioned soils today are available in most stores selling gardening equipment and supplies. However, I will explain the preparation of these soils as some of the readers may have difficulty in obtaining them.

It is not absolutely necessary to have bonsai soil as the basic soil. Any kind of soil will do if it has the required qualities that have been mentioned, such as little percentage of fertilizing elements (too much fertilizer at the start can *burn* a plant and kill it), good moisture-retention qualities, is granular and also able to absorb fertilizers satisfactorily. If the soil in your backyard meets these requirements, then it will do.

First prepare two kinds of soil: red loam or its equivalent and river sand—a slightly sticky granular soil and sand having a rough texture. Most bonsai can be raised with this combination. Therefore, all you have to do is just find the soil and sand that meet the requirements.

Red loam usually can be found about 3 feet down. River (or mountain) sand of the required quality usually can be found in the lower reaches of the river or in a volcanic mountain area.

After collecting this soil, expose it to strong sunlight and the wind in order to destroy the insect eggs that it may contain and also remove any harmful germs present. To be absolutely certain, you may sterilize the soil by using chloropicrin or Dithane.

Then the really small particles of soil must be removed with the aid of a sieve. These small particles must be removed because they can fill up the tiny spaces which serve as ventilation and drainage *passages*, and therefore have a bad effect on the plant you are trying to raise. The size of the grains of the soil you are using should be as nearly uniform as possible as this also brings good results.

It is convenient to have sieves with three different mesh sizes handy at all times. They can either be bought or you can make them yourself. Convenient mesh sizes are about $\frac{1}{16}$ inch $\frac{1}{8}$ inch and $\frac{3}{8}$ inch.

The soil should first be dried before you sift it, otherwise it may stick to the mesh, and red loam should first be crushed to break it down to the individual grains.

First use the $\frac{3}{8}$ inch sieve, proceeding to the smaller ones, keeping the earth sifted at each stage separate from the rest. Wooden boxes are satisfactory containers for this soil.

The largest-grained soil is known as *goro-tsuchi* about $\frac{3}{8}$ inch in diameter) and is placed in the bottom of the vessel you intend to use to ensure good drainage. The next-sized soil if used as the next layer, on which the roots of the plants are placed. The final, or surface layer, is made up of the next smaller sized grains. The small particles that were sifted through the $\frac{1}{16}$ inch screen are too small for use with bonsai and should be disposed of.

Let us now study the composition of the soils. Generally speaking, each plant has an affinity towards a certain quality of soil. Therefore one must prepare the mixture that best suits the plant one intends to raise. If you obtain your plant from its natural environment, study the type of soil that it has been growing in so that you will know which soil best suits it.

Do not mix too many kinds of soil, as this will only result in spoiling the characteristics of each soil. A mixture containing two, or three at the most, types of soil is entirely sufficient. The following are the more popular mixtures:

1.   *Coniferae*:   50 percent red loam and 50 percent sand, or 30 percent red loam and 70 percent sand, or 100 percent red loam.

2.   Other trees: 60 percent red loam, 30 percent sand and 10 percent leaf mold, or 70 percent red loam and 30 percent sand and artificial fertilizer.

3.   Flower and fruit plants: 50 percent red loam, 30 percent sand and 20 percent leaf mold.

The major purpose in training *coniferae* is to create the stately shape of a big old tree through control of unnecessary growth of the trunk and branches, or more simply, age it while retarding its growth. Thus the need for more than the 50 percent of sand in the soil mixture, whereas the other trees require more red loam as they need more moisture.

Soil used in raising plants that bear flowers and fruit require soil which provides plenty of moisture and fertilizer.

When mixing the soil, remember that it must provide good drainage, so remove all small grains by sifting.   Poor drainage results in making the vessel damp, circumvents proper ventilation and thereby causes the roots to decay.   Poor drainage affects even those plants which require large quantities of water.

4.   Tools for Transplanting (*Fig. 18*)

1)   Horticultural Shears: A light and sharp pair of these shears used to cut branches, roots and thin wires are recommended.   Be sure to keep them sharp and free of rust.   Japanese stores stocking gardening equipment sell various types of shears for trimming branches, cutting wires, nipping sprouts, cutting leaves, etc.

2)   Saw: Used when removing a large trunk, branch or root, one with small, sharp teeth is recommended.   If you are sawing *coniferae*

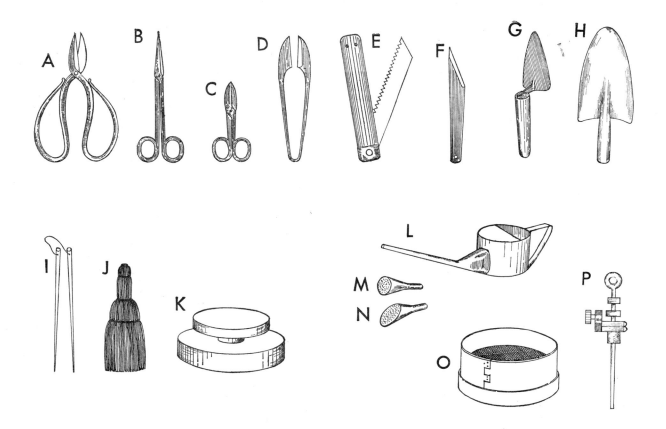

FIGURE 18. *Bonsai tools.* (A) *Pruning shears.* (B) *Sprout nip-ping shears.* (C) *Wire nipper.* (D) *Leaf-cutting shears.* (E) *Saw.* (F) *Knife.* (G) *Trowel.* (H) *Garden trowel.* (I) *Bamboo sticks.* (J) *Hemp palm broom.* (K) *Rotating table.* (L) *Watering can.* (M) *Cone-shaped rose for watering can.* (N) *Diagonal-faced cone-shaped rose.* (O) *Sieve.* (P) *Sprayer.*

or gummy trees, keep cotton wool and benzine handy to clean off any sticky substance adhering to the saw. This will make your work easier.

3) Knife: A knife is used to smooth off the severed end of a tree in order to facilitate easy conglutination. A long, thick and sharp-bladed knife is recommended.

4) Trowel: This is used to smooth the surface of the earth after the plant has been placed in a vessel. A thin, small trowel is sufficient. If one is not obtainable, the same results can be obtained with a piece of wooden board.

5) Garden Trowel: A small horticultural trowel used for various purposes, such as mixing soil, placing soil in the pot, etc.

6) Bamboo Chopsticks: A pair of these are indispensable when transplanting bonsai. Bamboo chopsticks about 1 foot long and with a thickness equivalent to a pencil are very handy when loosening old soil compressed around the roots of a plant, or when packing soil around the roots during transplantation.

7) Hemp Palm Broom: This is used when sweeping away soil scattered at the base of the bonsai trunk, or when smoothing the surface of the soil. A small one with soft tips is recommended.

8) Rotating Table: A small rotating table is handy to have as you can place the bonsai on it and move it around as you work on the plant. The table top should be large enough to accommodate the vessel and high enough to allow you to work freely while in a sitting position.

9) Watering Can: A very necessary item, it should have interchangeable roses for use with the various types of plants. More precisely, a rose with a flat face produces a fairly strong water pressure which reaches deeply into thick masses of leaves but is not suitable for newly-transplanted bonsai as it ruins the surface of the soil. A rose with a diagonal face, on the other hand, provides a softer spray. A half-gallon or gallon sized watering can is adequate.

10) Sieves: These are required for the preparation of pot earth. The three required mesh sizes are about $\frac{1}{16}$ inch, $\frac{1}{8}$ inch and $\frac{3}{8}$ inch.

These are the tools required in bonsai transplantation. In addition, a spray is needed when you sterilize the plants and water the leaves. Malleable copper wire also is required for use when making corrective adjustments of the distribution of branches. This latter process will be explained later in this volume.

5. Transplantation Procedures

When transplanting a bonsai, choose a bright sunny day during the suitable season that you have learned of earlier in this volume. However, you should choose a working area, either indoors or outdoors, where sunlight will not hit the plant directly. Be sure to have all the tools you need, as well as the equipment required for the purpose.

1) *Removal of the Bonsai Tree*

A tree which is to be transplanted should not be watered on the day preceding transplantation or the day of transplantation so that the soil will be kept fairly dry, and enable the plant to be simply unearthed.

First, lightly tap the outside wall of the vessel containing the plant, tilt the plant slightly and remove it. If the plant cannot be removed without any fuss or bother, then use a bamboo chopstick to loosen the earth around the plant, and then pull the plant out, together with the pot soil.

2) *Loosen Soil Around Roots*

Place the removed tree on the rotary table at an inclined angle.

First loosen the soil at the bottom with the bamboo chopsticks and then proceed up around the sides. In the case of a *coniferae*, about 30 to 40 percent of the soil should be removed, whereas for other plants about 50 percent should be removed. Even where the same specie of tree is concerned, more soil should be removed in the case of the younger trees, and less in the case of the older trees.

3) *Trimming the Roots*

After the soil is removed, use the horticultural shears to trim the roothair emerging from the remaining soil, as well as those roots which are decayed or too large to permit easy transplantation.

When trimming the taproot, it should be done so that its out end will face diagonally towards the bottom of the pot. The cut end also should be smoothed off, to prevent it from rotting. The scissors must be sharp or the cut end may be crushed, resulting in rot.

4) *Pruning Branches*

Prune and trim all unnecessary leaves and branches. This is done in order to maintain a proper balance between the amount of moisture taken in by the roots and that given off into the air by the leaves and branches. Trimming and pruning also helps to give the plant a good appearance.

5) *Plugging Hole in Vessel*

All bonsai vessels have a hole or holes in the bottom which serves both for ventilation and drainage. If the hole is left open, the pot soil is liable to run out through it, so some sort of stopper is used. Currently a vinyl net, or bark of hemp palm is used to cover the hole.

6) *Filling the Vessel*

For the bottom layer, use that part of the earth which did not pass through the sieve with the $\frac{3}{8}$ inch mesh. This will facilitate proper drainage. This layer should have a depth equal to 20 percent of the total depth, although it may vary slightly according to the shape of the vessel. The grains making up the soil should have a uniform size, and the soil should be dry.

7) *The Middle Layer*

The second layer should consist of the red granular soil that did not pass through the $\frac{1}{8}$ inch mesh of the sieve, or a mixture of the same red loam with river sand. The plant is then set upon this layer, the method of doing this to be explained later.

8) *Positioning the Plant*

Having *set* the plant, hold the trunk with one hand and with the other hand spread the roots in all directions. Then add the medium-sized granular soil until about 80 percent of the pot is filled. Next use the bamboo chopsticks to probe around the roots of the plant, lightly, to make certain that the earth is packed in well around the roots and there are no vacant spaces. Keep doing this, and adding soil if necessary, until the tree remains firmly upright. In the case of *coniferae*, the soil should be packed tighter than for other plants.

9) *Top Layer of Soil*

Spread a thin layer of the soil which did not pass through the $\frac{1}{16}$ inch mesh. Pile the soil up around the base of the trunk so that it forms a mound. The surface of the soil should be at least one-tenth of the height of the pot from the rim of the pot. Level the surface of the soil with a trowel or wooden board, and sweep all soil or sand off the trunk and elsewhere on the plant with a hemp palm broom.

10) *Sufficient Water*

Sprinkle water over the tree with the aid of a watering can having small nozzles. Keep sprinkling the plant until water runs out of the hole in the bottom of the pot. Let the water in the watering can warm up in the sunshine before sprinkling it over the plant.

After the transplantation is complete, the bonsai should be placed in a shaded spot protected from the wind for about two weeks.

Leaf-watering, or *hamizu*, (to be explained later) should be done two or three times a day. Then starting from the third week, the plant should be placed on an outdoor bonsai shelf. The frequency of watering should be reduced, the point being just to keep the roots of the plant moistened at all times. Too much water may result in the roots rotting or cool them unduly, causing a delay in their growth. Be sure to keep the bonsai out of the rain if the rain is heavy, or falls for a long period.

It takes from two to four weeks for the transplanted tree to take firm roots in its new home. Naturally this varies with the species. When it has firmly taken root, sprouts will begin to grow and you can then begin to expose the plant to the sun. However, it is too early to begin using fertilizer.

I shall now explain how the plant should be set in the vessel. The following explanation is a general one, because the difference in the distribution of a plant's branches and the general shape of the various trees do not permit a uniform rule.

Upright Attitude (*Chokkan*): Set the trunk at the center of the pot and a little to the rear, with a slight inclination towards the front of the pot.

Leaning Attitude (*Shakan*): If the trunk leans to the left, set it at the center of the vessel and closer to the right side, or vice versa, with a slight inclination towards the front of the vessel. A tree which has an extended branch pointing either left or right should be treated in the same manner.

Double Trunks (*Sokan*), Separate and Multiple Trunks from One Stock: Place them at the very center of the vessel.

Group (*Yoseue*) and Multiple Trunks Connected at the Roots (*Netsuranari*): These also should be placed in the center of the pot, and slight alterations made to adjust the shape of those not fully trained with those which have already been trained into a satisfactory shape.

Bonsai has a front and a back, and when it is placed in a pot, its front should be so placed that it will face the viewers.

Naturally, the next questions is: How does one tell the front of a bonsai from its back?

This depends on the distribution of the branches. In principle, it is not good to have the branches stretching forward. Rather, it is better to have them stretching towards the rear as this gives a sense of depth. On the other hand, it is best to have those roots which are exposed stretching forward. This creates an air of stability. Therefore, the front of a bonsai is determined by taking these points into consideration.

You must determine the front and back of the bonsai before you transplant it. Otherwise, you may ruin the tree by turning it around repeatedly, or pulling it out repeatedly in order to determine its best profile. Remember that the bonsai is a living thing and not a roomful of furniture.

3. Training

A BONSAI is an artistically trained wild plant.   So there is no meaning if you simply transplant a wild tree into a pot.   It is a living thing which transparently changes with the seasons, and it grows or it withers and dies.   To be more precise, if the plant is left alone, the branches with a higher percentage of vitality may just keep growing, at the expense of the smaller branches which would wither, thereby ruining the shape of the tree and greatly reducing, if not removing, its artistic value.

Constant care is therefore necessary in order to maintain the trained shape of the bonsai in excellent condition.   Since bonsai is the joint effort of man and nature, it is only natural that this object of art requires the utmost care.

Such training care is defined in bonsai terminology as *seishi*, which is one of the three major methods of bonsai culture, along with " material plant raising " and " transplantation."   A mistake in *seishi* will result in total failure, even if the material plant, or *araki*, is an excellent one. On the contrary, skillful training may result in a superb bonsai even if the *araki* is not of the best quality.

Among the practical *seishi* methods are *tekishin*, *sentei* and *harigane-kake*, or sprout nipping, pruning and wire hanging.   In addition, there are leaf cutting and branch hanging, or the correction of shape with the aid of a jack. Explanations on each method will be explained in this volume. However, each of them has a common trait, that is, the creation of artistic beauty through originality and skill coupled with utilization of the excellent qualities of the natural beauty contained in the material plant. The raising of bonsai requires an aesthetic sense, an essential prerequisite apart from horticultural skill, and therein lies both the difficulty and profound interest of bonsai raising.

1. PRINCIPLE OF TRAINING

It has been said that the master artists of bonsai trained their plants after the shape of excellently-shaped stately old trees that they had found during their roamings through the mountains and plains in search of exactly such trees. It is so true that we often see trees in their natural surroundings which particularly catch our eye, and that we find both fascinating and charming. A careful observation of such trees may be one way of improving our skills in bonsai raising.

However, bonsai, as I said earlier, is an artistic achievement rather than a tree in its natural state. In this sense, not a few bonsai horticulturalists have tried to train their trees into shapes that were inspired by paintings of trees.

In addition, there are many publications that carry pictures of bonsai masterpieces, and these serve as excellent reference material because they are bonsai that have been fully perfected. It is useful to study such pictures, not only because they are examples of good bonsai but also because they may give you some idea as to the numerous shapes possible. It also is advisable to study not only the pictures, but to learn the various techniques and skills needed with the aid of illustrated books.

You may also further improve your talents by taking in all the bonsai exhibitions available. As the old saying goes, " Seeing is believing." I would advise you to study as many bonsai masterpieces as possible, and visit bonsai experts and amateurs who own masterworks, in order to learn practical techniques as well as to enjoy the plants they possess. Remember that the ability to appreciate bonsai is as important as the ability to raise them.

Rapid improvement of your skill can only be achieved by raising a bonsai for yourself and learning the individual characteristics of trees. Nip sprouts, prune branches and apply wires by yourself as you learn the tricks of the hobby by means of books and instructions from well-versed bonsai horticulturalists. Do not give up after one or two failures and enjoy in learning as you learn to enjoy. These simple facts are the key to improvement. I shall now explain the principles of the training method.

1) First determine the shape and type of bonsai that you intend to train your material tree into. If you wish to feature a curved trunk, then you will have to train it so that the curvature of both trunk and branches is increased. If, in reverse, you wish to feature a straight trunk, then you will have to straighten any portion of the trunk that has a curve as you train the tree.

2) Thin out the distribution of the branches so that the over-all appearance of the bonsai can be seen at a glance. However, an excessive trimming of the branches will make the trunk too conspicuous and spoil the general appearance.

3) Branches jutting out toward the viewer do not help the bonsai's appearance and should be removed. Thin out the branches in front, while at the same time leaving the branches in the back virtually untouched so that their distribution suggests a sense of depth.

4) Either one of two branches which are growing in parallel or across each other should either be removed or trained to grow in another direction through the use of wiring.

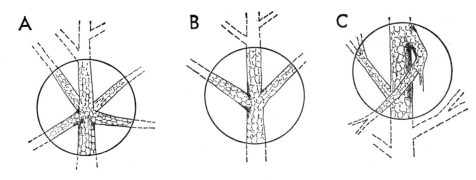

FIGURE 19. (A) "*Kuruma-eda.*" (B) "*Kannuki-eda.*"
(C) "*Futokoro-eda.*"

5) One of two branches on the same level but growing in opposite directions, and of the same length, should be removed.

6) Romove *kannuki-eka*, and *kuruma-eda* (See *Fig. 19*).

7) Cut off *futokoro-eda* (See also *Fig. 19*).

8) Trim the tips of branches which are too lively as compared to the others. The ends of the branches usually have the strongest vitality, and trimming the tips provides energy to spur smaller branches to growth.

9) In order to create the stately shape of an ancient tree, the branches growing on the lowest one-quarter of the tree must be cut off.

10) When shaping the tree, pull the branches down slightly with the use of wire so that the tree takes on an aged look.

These are some of the principles of *seishi*, but there always be some exception. In short, the most important point is that the bonsai must be trained into a shape that can be appreciated, and that in so doing unnecessary sections of the tree must be removed.

2.   HOW TO NIP SPROUTS

Sprout nipping is another important part of training a bonsai. The purpose of this is to prevent the plant from wasteful growth by nipping the buds, thereby resulting in shortening the distance between the joints of branches and assisting the growth of sub-branches.   Once the sprouts have been nipped, the new leaves that grow are smaller in size than normal.   It is in this way that the growth of small branches and tiny leaves, which constitute one of the important factors of a bonsai's aesthetic merits, are created.   The timing and the method of sprout nipping varies according with the species of tree or plant, some plants requiring the nipping process more than once.

The following are the major examples of sprout nipping:

1) Pine (except Five needle pine): During the period from late June to early July, when the new sprouts are fully grown, cut them off at their roots with your finger nails or a pair of scissors.   The season mentioned is standard for Tokyo, where the sprouts begin to emerge late in March or in early April, and grow rapidly during the next months.   A lively tree yields sprouts as long as 4 inches by June. They must be removed in their entirety from their base up (*Fig. 20-*1).

New sprouts begin to emerge about a month later, but they do not reach any size as their growth is checked by the cold weather making itself known.   This enables them to maintain a balance between the length of their leaves and the size of the bonsai tree.   Needless to say, the length of these second-growth leaves depends upon the local climate, setting the rule that nipping time in warm regions should take place later than in colder regions.

1.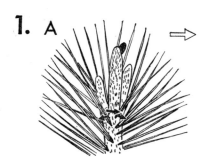

2.

3.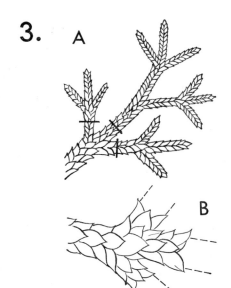

FIGURE 20. *How to nip sprouts.* 1. (A) *Japanese black pine—nip sprouts.* (B) *New-grown buds after sprouts were nipped.* 2. *Small ball-shaped buds of Cryptomeria and Common Ezo spruce should be nipped with tips of finger nails whenever they emerge.* 3. *Nip new shoots whenever they appear.* (A) *Growth of new leaves.* (B) *Nipping method.*

The growth rate of each sprout sometimes varies in accordance with the location of the branches on which they grow. For instance, where the sprouts on the upper branches may be as long as 3 inches, the sprouts on the lower branches will be only 1 inch long. In this event, nip the sprouts on the lower branches first, removing those on the upper branches about one or two weeks later.

This may sound strange to the uninitiated but there is a valid reason, and that is that the growth of the new sprouts on the lower branches, which have less vitality, will be hastened by the early removal. By the same token, if the stronger sprouts of the upper branches are removed later than the weaker sprouts on the lower branches, the former is forced to delay the growth of the new sprouts, thereby balancing the size of the second-growth sprouts on both the upper and lower branches.

2) Five Needle pine : Normally new sprouts are not removed. When this is done, the next crop of sprouts often fail to grow, or, if they do, they tend to vary in size and spoil the appearance of the tree. However, when there is a notable difference in the growth rate of the branches, a sprout at the tip of the branch showing excessive vitality had best be nipped off. In other words, those sprouts which are likely to spoil the shape of the tree, or those you believe to be unnecessary, must be removed before they grow too large.

3) Juniper, Cryptomeria, Common Ezo spruce : When leaves grow from the round buds, nip them off. However, the nipping of buds should not take place during the first year when a plant—which was collected in the wilderness and whose branches and roots have been well pruned—has not regained its normal vitality after the transplantation (*Fig. 20–2, 3*).

4) Sargent juniper, Hinoki cypress : Nip off Y-shaped sprouts no matter how many times they emerge. Some people tend to nip them off too deeply, digging into the roots of the sprouts. Be careful

to remove the sprout only, as, if they are nipped too deeply, these species often wither. They also tend to yield deformed leaves, especially in the case of Sargent juniper.

5) Apricot, Quince, Peach, Cherry trees : Sprouts of these flower-bearing trees should be left untouched until the end of June or the early part of July, when the newly developed branches which have grown to excess have to be pruned. If the pruning is done too early, new sprouts will make their appearance and the tree will not bear flowers the following year.

Fruit trees such as the English holly and Spindle tree should be treated in this manner also. However, in the case of those trees whose flowers or fruit are a key point of their appreciation, it is important that a considerable number of buds be left un-nipped.

6) Maple, Elm, etc. : Those you wish to train into trees having thick branches with soft delicate tips should have their sprouts removed repeatedly before they grow too big. Namely, in this particular case, repetitious nipping of sprouts is necessary during the period from the spring sprouting season to defoliation time in the autumn.

Lastly, there is one important point worthwhile mentioning in regard to the nipping of sprouts. That is, that the sprouts of trees which have not regained sufficient vitality due to an excessive pruning of its branches and roots at the time of transplantation, should not be nipped until such time as the trees have fully recovered. The nipping of sprouts is a must in connection with *seishi*, or the shaping of bonsai, but it always must be done with full consideration for the strength (vitality) of the tree.

3. LEAF-CUTTING METHOD

Leaf-cutting is one of the methods of tree shaping that is peculiar to Maple and Elm, which are required to be so trained that they have thickly distributed branches with soft delicate tips. But this method does not apply to *coniferae*.

About two months after a tree is transplanted, all the leaves are cut off at the center of the stalks with a pair of scissors. The remaining portion of the stalks will soon wither and fall, thus artificially creating the autumnal season when the trees shed their leaves. Two or three weeks later, new leaves will emerge from new sprouts.

In other words, one leaf-cutting will cause the tree to experience two autumns in one year, enabling it to spur the growth of its branches to an extend that would normally take two years. If the tree is a particularly healthy one, this process can be repeated two or three times a year. Needless to say, it should not be applied in the case of a weak tree.

In the case of Elm and Chinese elm, the leaves are cut off together with the tips of unnecessary newly-grown twigs, because it is quite troublesome to have to remove the leaves, which are so small and so numerous, one by one. When removing the leaves and twigs, the utmost care should be taken to protect the over-all shape of the tree.

A sufficient amount of fertilizer should be given the tree before the leaf-cutting takes place. After the leaf-cutting is completed the plant should then be thoroughly watered and placed under a reed screen or in some spot where it will be protected from strong sunshine and the wind. Spray water over the plant daily in order to expedite the sprouting. When the sprouts begin to make their appearance, move the bonsai to an outdoor shelf, spray water on it daily and feed it a weak solution of fertilizer so that it may regain its strength as quickly as possible.

As I stated previously, leaf-cutting should not be done when the tree is a weak one. This also applies in the case of the individual branches.

If the branch does not look strong, then leave it alone.

Adequate leaf-cutting will produce many small branches and small leaves, and result in the completion of a graceful bonsai.

4. PRUNING THE BRANCHES AND ROOTS

The pruning of branches and roots, known as *sentei* in Japanese bonsai terminology, is, along with wiring and the aforementioned sprout-nipping, one of the important *seishi* methods. An explanation of wiring will come later.

Why is the pruning of branches necessary? By removing unnecessary branches, the burden of the tree is lessened; it results in good ventilation and lighting, thereby hastening the tree's ramification; and the tree is given a beautiful over-all shape. In short, *sentei* is devoted to the creation of beauty in the form of a bonsai.

Now we come to the pruning of the roots. Old roots, decayed roots, and a taproot which is too long to facilitate setting of the plant in the pot during transplantation, must be removed to help hasten the generation of numerous new ciliary roots. This helps to maintain a balanced water supply for the trunks and the branches of the tree, the water being sucked up by the plant through its roots. This is very necessary for the upkeep of the plant's metabolism.

Generally the pruning of the roots takes place when the tree is being transplanted. When pruning of the roots is found to be insufficient for the purpose, then additional pruning of the branches must take place to supplement the root pruning during either the dormant season or the growing season. The basic rules regarding the pruning of branches have already been mentioned in the chapter dealing with *seishi*, or shaping, so I will explain here which branch should be pruned during the dormant season and which during the growing season.

Pruning During the Growing Season

Branches that have grown too long and mar the shape of the bonsai —called *tochoshi*, or excessively-grown branches—and the *futokoro-eda*, those small sub-branches densely growing inwards, are the only branches which should be pruned. This process is rarely used in the case of *coniferae* but other plants are often pruned in this manner.

The *tochoshi*, or excessively-grown branches, should be cut off at their very base, but, if they are overhealthy branches, a little portion of their base should be left. Then gradually trim this portion down so that no new sprouts will grow from that part of the trunk the branch was removed from. The *futokoro-eda* should be cut off at their base soon after they make their appearance.

Pruning During the Dormant Season

The dormant season is that period from late autumn to early spring. If you are going to prune your tree, severe winter cold should be avoided. During the dormant season, the remaining portions of the *tochoshi* pruned earlier, withered branches, and unnecessary branches among densely grown and distributed branches should be removed in such a manner as to help improve or maintain the over-all shape of the tree. An important point to remember in the case of trees that feature flowers, such as Apricot, Peach and Cherry, the branches should be pruned short in order to control the number of flowers on each branch and also to have them bear their flowers evenly.

A sharp blade should be used when pruning branches, and the exposed parts of thick branches and trunks where the cuts were made should be trimmed clean immediately to expedite quick recovery of the bark.

Pruning of Roots

All plants maintain themselves through their roots. Therefore, the growth of a tree is dependent on the condition of its roots, and there is a close relation between the roots, leaves and branches. The pruning of the roots during transplantation can prevent an excessive growth of leaves and branches, and also helps in shaping up the tree's appearance.

Roots are roughly divided into two categories—*hige-ne*, or ciliary roots, (root hairs), and *gobo-ne*, or taproots. The ciliary roots take in nutrition for the plant while the taproot burrows straight down deep into the earth and, with a few diverted sub-roots, contribute to the stability of the tree or plant.

When pruning roots, first cut short the taproot which is too long to fit into the bonsai vessel. Cut the root horizontally, and if you use a saw to do this, smooth the cut end with a sharp knife. Then trim the ciliary roots if there are too many of them, thus hindering an adequate flow of air and warmth (from sunshine) inside the vessel. Also remove those roots that may be withered or decayed. These steps prevent the tree from producing *tochoshi*, or excessively-grown branches, while at the same time facilitating the growth of new sub-branches.

The ciliary roots should not be exposed to the air for a long while when the tree is being transplanted. The plant should be handled quickly and transplanted as soon as possible because the plant may wither and die if the roots become too dry.

5. Wiring

Wiring is utilized in bonsai to shape the tree into the appearance required. The wire is used to control the shape and direction of the trunk and branches, making them grow in a curve where they are straight, or, in reverse, straightening them out where they curve. This is the most important, and most direct, aspect of the *seishi*, or shaping, method.

Generally this method is used when one is trying to train *araki*, or bonsai material, into a proper bonsai.

It also is used when one tries to change the over-all original shape of the bonsai into that which one considers as idealic. Another time it is used is when one is entirely satisfied with the shape of the plant in order that the plant will maintain that shape. This is done by wiring small branches that are likely to grow out in ways that would mar the shape of the plant. Whatever the reason this method is used is, the manner of so doing and the rules concerned are the same.

From a technical point of view, one needs to have a highly aesthetic eye and the technique of an expert. However, anyone can accomplish this wiring if they wish to train just a fairly good bonsai instead of a masterpiece, although it would be best if you could have some experienced person lend a hand.

The wire that is used for this purpose must be soft, easy to handle, and not so elastic that it is durable enough for repeated use. Best suited to these qualifications is copper wire. You should keep a supply of the wire in several thicknesses. Ordinarily the thicknesses vary from a No. 4 to a No. 24, with those from No. 12 to No. 18 being most frequently used.

No. 4 wire is strong enough to be used to bend a trunk with a diameter of $3\frac{1}{2}$ inches, while No. 24 is used to exert a pull on the tips of small branches. You have to use your judgement in this matter, using a wire of minimum thickness which yet is strong enough to ensure the forceful correction of a trunk or branch.

The wire must be annealed in a straw fire before it is used. This may sound absurd, but when this is done and the wire is wound around the branch or the trunk, it hardens to serve its purpose well. In addition, it will not injure the bark when being wound around the branch or trunk. For convenience, wind the annealed wire on a bobbin or a piece of wood and keep it in a dry place.

The time of year such wiring should take place varies with the type of plant. The best time of year for most plants is during the period from late October to late February. April-June is best for such trees as Pine. Weak trees, and those just transplanted, should not be wired.

First study the over-all appearance of the tree and then determine the shape you think will best suit the particular tree. Thoroughly prune unnecessary branches and leaves. Wiring must be started off with the trunk, proceeding then to the lower branches. The lowest branch is handled first, then its sub-branches, and then you proceed to the next branch, making your way up to the top branches in this manner.

When you wind the wire around a trunk or branches, lightly insert the end in some notch or place it in the ground at the base of the tree so that it will not race. Wind the wire diagonally around the trunk, and not too tightly, especially in the case of young, fast-growing trees, as the wire will cut into the bark and ruin it (*Figs. 21, 22*).

Before applying the wire to the trunk or branch, first take the trunk or branch between your fingers and softly bend it again and again till the desired shape is obtained. In the event this cannot be accomplished because of the hardness of the tree or because there is a fear that it will break if forcibly bent, make a very shallow cut on the trunk or branch where you wish to make the corrective bend before applying the wire. When wiring a tree that has weak and oversoft bark, first wrap the wire in paper.

The wire may be wrapped clockwise or counterclockwise, and you can apply two strands of wire if you wish a stronger effect. Do not, however, apply them in a crisscross manner as it will be less effective and also spoil the general appearance. When you have wrapped the

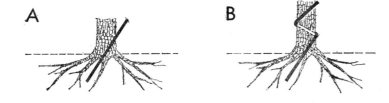

FIGURE 21. (A) *Thrust end of wire deep into soil so it will not spring free.* (B) *Wind wire around trunk so that it will not come loose.*

FIGURE 22. *When applying wire to a branch, anchor the wire at the base of the branch.* (A) *Front view.* (B) *Back view.*

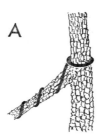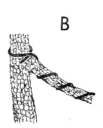

wire around the trunk in the form of a spiraling coil, make your corrective bend by slowly twisting it in a clockwise direction if you have applied the wire in this fashion, or vice versa.

To correct a thick trunk, first apply hemp string and then add pieces of thick copper wire in parallel with the stretch of the trunk. Then wind copper wire of less thickness around this to make the corrective bend. A lever and a jack are sometimes used for this purpose.

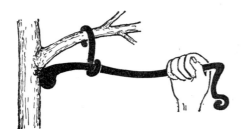

FIGURE 23.   *How to apply leverage.*

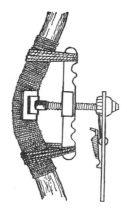

FIGURE 24.   *How to apply a jack.   Use hemp string to protect the bark, and place a bit of rubber under the jack.*

To make a correction in the shape of a trunk or branch with the aid of a lever, affix the ends of a rope or string like a sling on either side of the part to be corrected.   If you will have to exert a lot of pressure, the item should be wrapped in hemp rope and covered with wiring. Place your lever in the sling and apply pressure away from the trunk or branch you are correcting (*Fig. 23*).

If you plan to use a jack, bind hemp rope around that part you wish to bend, also setting a rubber pad between the tree and the end of the jack where pressure will be applied (*Fig. 24*).

If either of the two methods are used, the correction should be carried out in February when the tree does not yield sap.

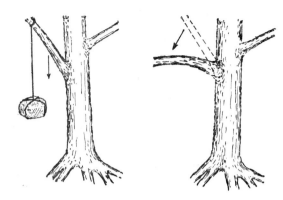

FIGURE 25. *Branch hanging method. Gradually bend the branch downwards with the aid of a weighted string.*

A bonsai that has been wired should be kept under a reed screen to protect it from direct sunlight for about three to four days. Sprinkle the leaves with water every day to give the plant a resting period before it is taken outdoors. The bonsai should also be kept out of strong winds as the trunk and branches sometimes develop small but invisible splits after wiring takes place.

As with everything else, the type of tree and the thickness of the trunk and branches control the period of time the wiring should be left alone before removal. Generally speaking, though, the smaller branches should be left wired for two to three months, and the larger branches for three to four months. If you can leave the wiring on the tree for about a year, the result would be perfect, unless the wire begins to cut into the bark of the tree.

6. How to " Hang " Branches

This is a very simple process. If you wish a branch to *hang*, just tie a piece of string with a weight on its end to the tip of the branch (*Fig. 25*).

This was a favorite technique of bonsai horticulturalists during the Meiji Era (1867–1912) who were not overly fond of the wiring method. Today people use this method when trying to shape a particularly sensitive tree or when they are not too confident of their ability to use the wiring method. In any case, this is the safest and simplest way, the best season for it being during the May-July period.

This method of *hanging* the branches can also be used to bend them in any direction you may desire. Simply affix a string or rope on the branch you wish to shape, and attach the other end to some other part of the tree so that you achieve the desired bend in the branch you are correcting. This is quite sufficient in fixing a branch as desired.

4. Maintenance and control

ONE often hears the expression, " I love bonsai, but they tend to wither. That is what troubles me." Is this really so? No, because bonsai won't wither that easily. They don't just wither on their own initiative, but rather it is you that have forced them to wither. I wish to impress you with this grave fact.

A bonsai is a living thing, and it will wither and die despite its struggle for survival if it is left without the necessary water, fertilizer and other care. In reverse, a physiological imbalance brought about by excessive watering and fertilizing also will result in the plant's withering and dying. In short, if the bonsai is handled with the proper care by loving hands, it will not wither and die, but instead improve itself year after year.

I will therefore set forth in this chapter a summary of the general knowledge that is required in the maintenance of a bonsai.

A love and appreciation of bonsai is, naturally, of prime importance, but at the same time you should have a fairly good knowledge regarding the care of a bonsai. Without such knowledge, one's affection for bonsai will be ineffective and result only in failure.

1. WHERE TO KEEP BONSAI

The general conditions regarding the placement of a bonsai are as follows :

1. The spot must be sunny throughout the year, isolated from the afternoon sun during the summer, and must be comparatively warm in winter.

2. The site must be assured of a proper flow of air and yet be protected from strong winds.

3. It must be a clean spot, free from dust, soot and smoke.

4. It should not be close to railway lines or roads which would cause vibrations.

5. The spot should be one where you will find it convenient to water the plant, nip the sprouts or feed it fertilizer.

6. It should be inaccessible to cats and dogs.

For example, an ideal spot would be a suburban one facing towards the south, with an open space to the southeast and a building, or woods, or some barrier to check the north winds. Being rather difficult to find such a spot in an urban area, a section of a small garden, or a veranda will suffice. However, either should meet the requirements listed above as closely as possible.

A classic Japanese horticultural statement says " Five days of wind and ten days of rain," signifying that best conditions for a plant's growth is plenty of rain and fresh air, in addition to sunshine. In fact, it is necessary to provide the plant with plenty of sun and air, and to expose it to the rain (light) and dew.

If the plant does not receive sufficient sunshine, its new leaves will be weakened, as will the entire plant, leaving it vulnerable to disease. Trees growing in a spot where there is no wind at all often are badly damaged by insects. *Coniferae* sometimes grow compact leaves when exposed to the wind. The benefits of the rain and dew hardly need to be explained, other than to say that they also help to keep the plant clean, especially in the urban areas.

As strong, afternoon sunshine is apt to *burn* the leaves, it should be avoided. A reed screen will accomplish this if the natural environment won't. Strong winds also can hurt the leaves, and at worst can break branches or blow the whole bonsai off the shelf where it is being kept. If heavy winds are expected, be sure to anchor the bonsai to the shelf with wire or string. Heavy, or continuous rainfall will result in decaying of the roots, so place the bonsai under some type of shelter.

With the exception of *coniferae*, which are strongly resistant to cold, plants should be carefully protected from the cold in winter. Naturally, if your area is one where the winter cold can be very bitter, the *coniferae* also should be protected. The trees are liable to weaken, if not wither, and the bonsai vessel may break when the vessel earth is frozen.

Therefore you are advised to select a spot facing the sun and which is sheltered from the north. If possible, a greenhouse type of structure would be ideal, but if this is impossible then built a long eaves on the south side of your building and place the bonsai under it to protect them from the snow and frost. Cover the vessel earth with straw to help it retain the heat.

2. BONSAI SHELF AND STALL

It is best not to place the bonsai directly on the ground, otherwise the tree and vessel may get dirty from splashed mud and dirt during a heavy rain. In addition, those trees with thickly-developed branches cannot obtain a sufficient supply of air; there is a tendency for the hole at the bottom of the vessel to become blocked hindering drainage; and it makes access to the tree easier for such nuisances as ants, earthworms and slugs.

It also is bad to place a bonsai directly on a stone or on concrete, for the plant is chilled in winter and in summer is dried out by the radiation of heat. Therefore, because of all the foregoing reasons, a bonsai must be kept on a shelf or a stall.

Bonsai Shelf

Shelves should not be so big that they cannot be moved around. Although shelves affixed to wooden fences also are used, the mobile type is much better. This is simple to understand, as the sun shines from different directions in the different seasons and changes are apt to take place in the immediate surroundings also. If the shelves can be shifted, there will be no loss to the bonsai.

The shelf should be 2 to 2½ feet high and from 8 inches to 3 feet in width. The length of the shelf will depend on the space available. The legs of the shelf can be made either from wood or cement, but whatever the material used, they must be strong enough to bear a considerable weight and have lasting durability.

When more than two boards are placed side by side to make a large shelf, there should be at least a ½ inch space between the boards. This will serve ventilation and drainage. Boards one inch thick are most suitable for this purpose.

The simplest shelf can be made out of two stones with flat surfaces, and a board. If the board is 3 feet or longer, another stone would help to make it more stable (*Fig. 26*).

Bonsai Stall

Kengai, or bonsai of the drooping-down style, is usually placed on top of a board affixed to the top of a log that has been driven upright

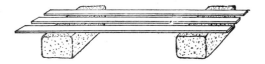

into the ground. There is no rule regarding the height of a stall other than that it should be high enough to provide good ventilation. Keep the bonsai vessel securely affixed to the stall, and move it to a safe place when strong winds are expected. Place stalls at different places in your garden and make them of varying heights so that they will enhance the general appearance of the area.

Wooden material used to construct the stall must be of good quality, and treated with varnish to prevent it from rotting.

3. How to Water Bonsai

It is a simple fact that plants not provided water will wither. Water is the most important element among the many factors involved in the care of bonsai throughout the year. There are, however, certain rules governing this. An overabundance of water spurs an excessive growth of the tree which can mar its shape, or it often leads to the death of the plant through decayed roots.

A simple rule to remember is, " Water the plant when the pot earth dries." Watering the plant when the earth is still wet or after the earth has dried out does not do the plant any good, and rather harms it.

Common mistakes by bonsai beginners are usually the excessive watering of the plants, rather than a failure to give them sufficient water. This is because the beginner fears that the plant may otherwise wither and die. Often the surface of the earth may look dry while the inner earth is filled with a great deal of moisture. Watering the plant under these conditions will only result in harmful effects.

Regardless of the time of year, the water you use for the bonsai should be as warm as the pot earth. That is, it should be water warmed by the sun. Rain water, well water or clean river water are said to be best, but in the cities your only choice is tap water. And there's no harm in that. Water must be soft. Dirty water or water containing too much acid must be avoided.

You are advised to prepare a watering can with two interchangeable roses for showering and sprinkling. Do not use a hose to water plants as it will only wash away the top soil in the pot and expose the roots. Use the watering can with a showering nozzle and gently pour water at the base of the tree.

The frequency involved in watering a plant may vary according to the seasons of the year, the type of tree, the soil, and the size of the vessel. However, the major difference lies in the season and the species of tree. In regard to the latter, there is a table attached to the end of this volume. Here I shall explain the seasonal changes in watering and the care involved.

New branches grow in April and May, and the plants, regardless of their type, need plenty of nutrition. So water and fertilizer are very important to the plants. If you let the earth in the vessel go completely dry, new buds will wither and stop growing, and even if the plant survives it will not be able to grow normally.

As a bonsai quickly adapts itself to routine habits, you are advised to water it regularly. If you give the plant too much water in these seasons, it will require more water than usual in the hot summer season when it is liable to suffer from a shortage of water. In other words, supply the plant with sufficient water regularly, avoiding excess. In fact, it might be better for the amount to be slightly wanting, rather than an excess.

Do not leave the plant out in the open if it rains heavily as the pot soil will absorb too much moisture, causing decay in the roots and spurring the growth of leaves at the same time, both facts harmful to the plant.

In the summer, you should water the plant at least twice a day, once in the morning and again in the late afternoon. A quick sprinkling with the watering can will not do, as the plant gets an insufficient, and thereby ineffective, amount. The correct way is to pour water around the base of the trunk until water runs out of the hole in the base of the vessel. Then sprinkle about the same amount of water over the plant. This will provide enough water for the soil to absorb, and also minimize the number of times a day the plant should be watered.

In addition to the regular watering, you should also carry out *hamizu*, or leaf sprinkling, in the summer. Especially in the cities where there is a great deal of smoke and soot in the air should this be done daily in the late afternoon. This will refresh the leaves and give the bonsai a cool appearance. Use a watering can with small nozzles and sprinkle water over the leaves until they get wet. A lesser amount of water than during an ordinary watering will suffice. Never do this in the noon hours as the drops of water on the leaves act as lenses for the sun and result in the leaves being burned. A reed screen may help to reduce the plant's dryness in the summer.

No particular caution is necessary when watering the plants in the autumn. Just keep them regularly watered.

A little care must be exercised in the winter. Naturally, the plant does not require watering as often as during the other seasons of the year. However, people often forget to water the bonsai as they dry up very slowly, and the tree suffers as a result. But please avoid excessive watering. If the soil in the pot contains too much moisture, it will become a potful of ice when the temperature goes down and freezes the water. So try to maintain a proper balance of moisture in the soil. Watering should take place between 10 a.m. and noon, or during the warmest time of the day.

In general, coniferous trees need less watering than other plant species.

4. FERTILIZERS

Bonsai can survive without fertilizer for about a year. After this, however, it begins to wither, starting with the leaves, then the twigs, branches and lastly the trunk. Plants living in a natural environment can freely develop their roots and absorb as much nourishment as they require. The bonsai is not able to do this, living in a very limited area, and therefore can not survive without an artificial supply of nutrition. You can well see why fertilizer is such an absolute necessity for bonsai.

There is no general rule in regard to the supply of fertilizer for bonsai. The amount each plant requires is dependent on the size of the pot, the type of plant and the difference in soil.

For instance, *coniferae* must be fed a continuous supply of fertilizer as it has leaves throughout the year. On the other hand, plants that feature flowers and fruit should be given fertilizer before and after the blooming, or ripening season. In the latter case, continuous supplying of fertilizer would only result in harmful effects.

Elm and Maple trees require a great deal of fertilizer during the spring budding season, but during the dormant season when they have shed their leaves, they do not require fertilizer. If they are supplied with fertilizer, the result may be a rotting of their roots.

Vital nourishment for any plant, including bonsai, includes nitrogen, phosphoric acid and potassium, chemicals commonly referred to as the three major elements of fertilizers. In addition to these, sulphur, lime, iron and salt also are required for the growth of the plant, but as these are usually found in soil and are not required in large quantities, there is no particular need to add them artificially. Transplantation every one or two years should be sufficient to ensure that the plant receives the required amount of these chemicals. However, the one thing the bonsai raiser must do is supply nitrogen, phosphoric acid and potassium.

Among various fertilizers used by Japanese bonsai horticulturalists the most popular one is known as *aburakasu*, or oil cake, which is available in shops. However, since it is composed mainly of nitrogen, it is good where the growth of leaves is concerned but lacks the potassium and phosphoric acid required by those plants which bear fruits and flowers.

If you wish your bonsai to produce many flowers or yield fruit, provided naturally that your plant is the right type, you will have to provide your plant with additional supplies of phosphoric acid and potassium.

The simplest way to give *aburakasu* to your plant is to place chunks about one inch in diameter on top of the plant soil. Then whenever you water the plant, the chinks of fertilizer will become damp and gradually melt into the soil. This is the easiest method. However, if it should rain continually, be careful because the broken chunks of fertilizer may possibly mar the appearance of the top soil.

Another way to feed the fertilizer to the plant is to dissolve it in water first. It is commonly acknowledged that liquid fertilizer made in the wintertime is especially good for plants. Dissolve about 1.8 liters of *aburakasu* in a five gallon can filled with water and keep it like that until fertilizer feeding time comes around the following spring.

Scoop out the upper portion of the mixture and weaken it with water on a one part solution-nine part water basis. The *demerits* of this system is that it takes a long time for preparation, and it also does not look very sanitary.

Recently however, a product called Hyponex has been introduced on the market which contains the proper amount of nitrogen, water soluble phosphoric acid and potassium. It also is very easy to handle, does not have a distasteful smell and has a clean appearance.

Hyponex can be dissolved in water quite easily so that there is no fear of an imbalance in the proportion of the various compounds or an excessive amount of fertilizer.

Dissolve one spoonful (about four or five grams) of Hyponex in one gallon of water, stirring it well for about five minutes. Then spread the mixture over the total area of the top of the soil in the bonsai vessel.

The time to supply plants with fertilizer varies with the type of plant. However, generally speaking, the plant should be so supplied once or twice a month during the springtime when it begins to bud.

Avoid the rainy season. After that feed the plant regularly at intervals of two to four weeks. Gradually lessen the frequency of feeding after September and then stop altogether when winter comes.

You must practice great care when supplying the bonsai with fertilizer as an excess of fertilizer will result in an excessive growth of leaves, and thereby lead to harm. Carefully watch the state of the bonsai before you supply it with fertilizer.

As Hyponex spurs the growth of the plant remarkably, be liberal in its application where weak plants are concerned. But use it sparingly where ordinary bonsai are concerned. Do not feed the bonsai with fertilizers immediately after transplantation, but give the plant sufficient time to develop new roots.

GUIDE TO 50 POPULAR SPECIES
OF BONSAI TREE

Information given in the following order:

(1) Common English names (Scientific names) (2) Watering
(3) Fertilization (4) Sprout-nippings, Pruning
(5) Wiring (6) Transplantation
(7) Pot soil (8) Notes

1. (1) Japanese black pine. (*Pinus thunbergii* Parl.) (2) Expose to sunshine but water sparingly. Leaf-watering in summer. (3) March, April, Oct. (4) Nip sprouts in April-May. Prune branches in March and Sept. (5) March-April. (6) Every three or four years, in March or April. (7) Red loam, or mix with sand (30%). (8) Remove old leaves in Sept.

2. (1) Japanese red pine. (*Pinus densiflora* Sieb. et Zucc.) (2)–(7) Same as in **1.** (8) Increase number of twigs and branches by nipping sprouts.

3. (1) Five needle pine; Japanese white pine. (*Pinus pentaphylla* Mayr.) (2) Same as in **1.** Supply sufficient leaf-watering. (3) Once a month in April, May, Sept., Oct. (4) Nip sprouts in May-June. Prune branches in March or Sept. (5)–(7) Same as in **1.** (8) Pack the soil quite firmly when transplanting.

4. (1) Common Ezo spruce; fir; Edo spruce; Yedo or Yesso spruce. (*Picea glehnii* Mast.) (2) Water sparingly. Leaf-water. (3) Same as in **3.** (4) Nip sprouts frequently during April-June. Prune branches in winter. (5) Nov.-Feb. (6), (7) Same as in **1.** (8) Keep in shade after transplantation.

5. (1) Common cryptomeria. (*C. japonica* D. Don.) (2) Give more water than usual. Leaf-water frequently. (3) Once a month in March, April, Sept., Oct. (4) Nip sprouts in spring and autumn. Prune branches in Feb.-March. (5) March. (6) Same as in **1.** (7) Black loam 50%, sand 30%, leaf mold 20%. (8) Use nothing except tips of your nails when nipping sprouts. Cryptomeria " abhor " metals.

6. (1) Needle juniper. (*Jupriperus rigida* Sieb. et Zucc.) (2) Water sparingly. Leaf-water in summer. (3) Once a month in April, May, Oct. (4) Nip sprouts occasionally in spring-autumn period. Prune branches in March. (5) Same as in **5**. (6) Same as in **1**. (7) Red loam 50%, sand 50%.

7. (1) Siebold hemlock. (*Tsuga siiboldii* Carr.) (2) Water sparingly. Leaf-water. (3) Once a month in March, Oct. (4) Nip sprouts in May, June. Prune branches in March or Oct. (5) Same as in **5**. (6) Same as in **1**. (7) Same as in **6**.

8. (1) Torreya. (*T. nucifera* Sieb. et Zucc.) (2) Water sparingly. Leaf-water in summer. (3) Same as in **6**. (4) Same as in **7**. (5) Same as in **5**. (6) Same as in **1**. (7) Same as in **6**. (8) Same as in **5**.

9. (1) Sargent juniper. (*Juniperus chinensis* L. var. *sargentii* Henry.) (2) Water sufficiently. Leaf-water frequently. (3) Once a month in March, April, May, Sept., Oct., Nov. (4) Nip sprouts in spring and autumn. Prune branches in March. (5) Feb.-March. (6) Every two years in March-April. (7) Red loam 50%, sand 50%, (8) Spray insecticide in March-April.

10. (1) Hinoki cypress. (*Chamaecyparis obtusa* Endl.) (2) Water sufficiently. No leaf-watering. (3) Once a month in March, April, May, Sept., Oct., Nov. (4) Nip sprouts occasionally during spring-autumn. Prune branches in autumn. (5) March or Oct. (6) Every other year in March-April. (7) Black loam 50%, sand 30%, leaf mold 20%. (8) Nip sprouts with tips of your nails. Avoid afternoon sun in summer.

11. (1) Oriental arborvita. (*Thuja orientalis* L.

(2) Water sparingly. Expose to night dew in summer. (3) Once a month in April, Oct. (4) Nip sprouts in May, Sept. Prune branches in autumn. (5) Same as in **10**. (6) Every two or three years in March or April. (7) Red loam 70%, sand 30%. (8) Avoid excessive watering.

12. (1) Japanese maple; Japanese mountain maple. (*Acer palmatum* Thunb.) (2) Once or twice a day in spring and autumn. Two or three times a day in summer. (3) Once or twice a month during March-May. (4) Nip sprouts wherever they grow. Prune the branches immediately before transplantation. (5) April-May. Cover wire with paper. (6) Every year in March. (7) *Kuropoka*, or mix it with 20% sand. (8) Nip sprouts frequently.

13. (1) Wax. (*Rhus succedanae* L.) (2), (3) Same as in **12**. (4) Remove twigs when sprouts are fully grown, leaving the lowermost two leaves, and let the tree grow new buds. (5) March. New branches in July. (6) Same as in **12**. (7) Black loam 50%, red loam 20%, sand 20%, leaf mold 10%. (8) Avoid afternoon summer sun.

14. (1) Thunberg barberry; Coral barberry. (*Berberis thunbergii* DC.) (2) Same as in **12**, but leaf-water in summer. (3) Once or twice a month in March-May, Sept. (4) As frequently as possible. (5) March. (6) Same as in **12**. (7) Black loam 50%, red loam 30%, sand 20%. (8) Cutting is good for propagation of this species.

15. (1) Japanese grey-bark elm; Saw-leaved zelkova. (*Z. serrata* Makino.) (2) Water sufficiently. Leaf-water in summer. (3) Once or twice a month in March-May. (4) Same as in **14**. (5) In June-July. Cover wire with paper. (6) Annually in March-April. (7) *Kuropoka*. (8) Avoid summer afternoon sun. Keep indoors in winter.

16. (1) Chinese hackberry. (*Celtis sinensis* Pers. var. *japonica* Nakai.) (2) Same as in **15**. (3) Same as in **15**, but use water sparingly. (4) Leave lowermost pair of leaves when nipping sprouts. Prune branches in autumn. (5), (6) Same as in **15**. (7) Black loam 60%, red loam 30%, sand 10%. (8) Excess fertilizer hardens branches.

17. (1) Crenata beech; White beech. (*Fagus crenata* Blume.) (2) Once or twice daily during spring and autumn, and two to three times daily in the summer. Expose plant to night dew. (3) Same as in **15**. (4) Nip side shoots once after they emerge. Leaf-cutting in summer. (5) March. (6) Same as in **15**. (7) Red loam 50%, *kuropoka* 30%, sand 20%. (8) Avoid direct sunshine in summer.

18. (1) Oak. (*Quercus serrata* Thunb.) (2) Supply plant with plenty of sunshine and water. (3) Same as in **15**. (4) Nip all sprouts, leaving two of three leaves on each. Prune branches when transplanting. (5) June-July. (6) Same as in **15**. (7) Same as in **17**.

19. (1) Chinese elm. (*Ulmus parvifolia* Jacq.) (2) Water sufficiently. Leaf-water in summer. (3) Same as in **15**. (4) Nip sprouts whenever they show. Approximately three or four times until July. (5) July. (6) March-April every year. (7) Black loam 50%, red loam 30%, sand 20%.

20. (1) Red-leafed hornbeam; Loose-flower hornbeam. (*Carpinus laxiflora* Blume.) (2) Same as in **19**. (3) Two or three times a month in March, April, May. (4) No sprout nipping or leaf-cutting. Prune branches in autumn. (5) At time of transplantation. (6), (7) Same as in **19**. (8) Take care not to let plant dry in summer.

21. (1) Mulberry. (*Morus alba* L.) (2) Twice a day in spring and autumn. Two to three times a day in summer. Expose to night dew. (3) Two

to three times a month during March-July. (4) Nip sprouts when they have grown $\frac{1}{2}$ inch in length. Prune branches in March. (5) Same as in **20**. Cover wire with paper. (6) Annually in April. (7) Black loam 50%, red loam 20%, leaf mold 20%, sand 10%. (8) Don't prune long roots at the time of transplantation. Wind them up and place them in the bonsai vessel.

22. (1) White birch. (*Betula tauschii* Koidz.) (2) Water sufficiently. Leaf-water. Avoid afternoon summer sun. (3) Same as in **21**. (4) Keep nipping sprouts, leaving two or three leaves, until June. (5) June. (6) Same as in **21**. (7) Black loam 60%, red loam 20%, sand 20%. (8) Keep plant where air is clean, otherwise bark darkens.

23. (1) Maidenhair. (*Ginkgo biloba* L.) (2) Normal. Expose to night dew. (3) Once a month during March-July. (4) Nip sprouts once in spring. Prune branches when transplanting. (5) Same as in **22**. (6) Annually in March-April. (7) Black loam 50%, red loam 20%, sand 30%.

24. (1) Trident maple. (*Acer buergerianum* Mig.) (2) Once or twice daily in Spring and autumn. Two or three times daily in summer. Avoid afternoon summer sun. (3) Same as in **12**. (4) Remove side shoots, leaving the two lowermost leaves. Leaf-cutting in June. Prune branches when transplanting. (5) June. (6) Annually in March. (7) Red loam 40%, *kuropoka* 30%, sand 30%. (8) Expose sufficiently to sun's direct rays in spring and autumn.

25. (1) Japanese flowering apricot. (*Prunus mume* Sieb. et Zucc.) (2) Water sufficiently whenever the surface of the pot soil takes on a whitish dry hue. Spray water on the flower buds. (3) Twice a month in May, June. Three times a month in July, Aug., Sept. (4) Prune old branches after flowers wither. Trim new sprouts when they

are fully grown. (5) June. "Hanging" recommended. (6) Annually in March when flowers wither. (7) Red loam 40%, *kuropoka* 30%, sand 30%. (8) Watch for harmful insects. Never pour water on the flowers.

26. (1) Winter jasmine; Naked flower jasmine. (*Jusminum nudiflorum* Lindl.) (2) Provide plenty of sunshine, sufficient water. (3) Once or twice monthly in April-Oct. except for July, Aug. (4) Nip unnecessary sprouts in June. (5) June. (6) Annually in March or Sept. (7) Black loam 50%, *kuropoka* 30%, sand 20%.

27. (1) Flowering quince. (*Chaenomeles lagenaria* Koidz.) (2) Same as in **26.** (3) Once or twice a month in March-Oct. (4)–(6) Same as in **26.** (7) Black loam 50%, red loam 30%, sand 20%. (8) Thin out excessive flower buds.

28. (1) Hall crab; Hall's crab-apple. (*Malus halliana* Koehne.) (2) Water sufficiently. Keep in a sunny place. (3) Same as in **27.** (4) Nip sprouts in May-June. Prune branches when flowers wither. (5) Sept. (6) Annually in March. (7) Black loam 70%, red loam 20%, sand 10%.

29. (1) Peach. (*Prunus persica* Batsch.) (2) Same as in **28.** (3) Once a month in March-Oct. (4) Prune branches shortly after flowers wither. Nip sprouts in June. (5) June. (6) Annually in March or Sept.-Oct. (7) Same as in **28.** (8) Tends to weaken during the cold weather.

30. (1) Cherry. (*Prunus Jamasakura* Sieb.) (2) Water sparingly. (3) Once a month in March-Sept. (4) Same as in **29.** (5) In May-June. Cover wire with paper. (6) Same as in **29.** (7) *Kuropoka* 40%, red loam 30%, Sand 30%. (8) Watch for harmful insects.

31. (1) Common camellia; Garden camellia. (*C. japonica* L. var. *hortensis* Makino.) (2) Normal.

Avoid afternoon summer sun. (3) Once a month in March-Oct. period except for July and Aug. (4) Prune the branches short when transplanting. Nip buds before July. (5) Same as in **30.** (6) Annually in March-May. (7) Black loam 70%, red loam 30%. (8) Keep indoors in winter.

32. (1) Lily magnolia; Japanese magnolia. (*M. liliflora* Desr.) (2) Water sufficiently. Avoid afternoon summer sun. (3) Twice a month in March-June. (4) Keep removing sprouts until June. Prune unnecessary branches. (5) June. (6) After flowers wither. (7) Black loam 60%, red loam 30%, sand 10%.

33. (1) Kobus magnolia. (*M. Kobus* DC.) (2), (3) Same as in **32.** (4) Prune branches when transplanting. Nip sprouts before July. (5)–(7) Same as in **32.** (8) Supply fertilizer until July.

34. (1) Korean bushcherry. (*Prunus tomentosa* Thunb.) (2) Normal. Provide plenty of sunshine. (3) Once or twice a month in March-Oct. (4) Nip sprouts and prune branches before July. (5) April. Cover wire with paper. (6) Annually in March. (7) Same as in **33.** (8) Plant weakens in cold weather.

35. (1) Common white jasmine. (*Jasminum officinale* L.) (2) Sufficiently. Avoid afternoon summer sun. (3) Once a month in April, May, Sept., Oct. (4) Same as in **34.** (5) June. Cover wire with paper. (6) Annually in March-April. (7) Black loam 50%, red loam 30%, leaf mold 10%, sand 10%. (8) Watch for excessive growth of branches.

36. (1) Gardenia. (*Gardenia jasminoides* Ellis. f. *grandiflora* Makino.) (2) Water sparingly. Provide plenty of sunshine. (3) Once a month in March-Oct. (4) Nip sprouts before July. Prune branches in autumn. (5) In May-June. (6) Annually in March-April or Sept. (7) Black loam 50%, red loam 30%, sand 20%. (8) Easily propagated by cutting and grafting methods.

37. (1) Satsuki azalea. (*Rhododendron lateritium* planch.) (2) Provide sufficient water, sun's rays. Leaf-water in summer. (3) Once a month except the flowering season and winter. (4) Nip sprouts, leaving two or three leaves. (5) Any time except the blooming season. Cover wire with paper. (6) Once annually after flowers wither. (7) *Kanumatsuchi* 70% mixed with crushed sphagna 30%. (8) Leaf-water for some time after transplantation. Avoid afternoon summer sun.

38. (1) Japanese wisteria. (*Wistaria floribunda* DC.) (2) Provide sufficient water and sunshine. (3) Once a month until July after the flowers wither. (4) Prune branches short after the blooming season and June, July, and Sept. (5) After blooming season. Cover wire with paper. (6) Annually in March. (7) *Kuropoka* 30%, leaf mold 30%, *kanuma-tsuchi* 20%, red loam 20%. (8) Do not cut the major root (tap root).

39. (1) Leatherleaf rhododendron. (*R. metternichii* Sieb. et Zucc.) (2) Water sufficiently. Expose to night dew. (3) Once a month in March-Sept. (4) Nip sprouts before July. Prune branches when transplanting. (5) July. Cover wire with paper. (6) Every other year, either in April or Oct. (7) *Kanuma-tsuchi* 40%, leaf mold 30%, sphagna 20%, red loam 10%.

40. (1) Common crape-myrtle. (*Lagerstroemia indica* L.) (2) Once a day in spring and autumn. Twice daily in summer. (3) Once a month in May-July. (4) Nip sprouts in March and after blooming season. Prune in March. (5) Mid-July. Cover wire with paper. (6) Annually in April. (7) *Kuropoka* 40%, red loam 40%, sand 20%. (8) Keep indoors in winter.

41. (1) Sweet osmanthus. (*O. asiaticus* Nakai.) (2) Water sparingly. Avoid afternoon summer sun. (3) Once a month in April-Sept. (4) Nip sprouts before mid-June. Prune branches when transplanting. (5) June. Cover wire with paper. (6) Annually in March. (7) Red loam 40%, black loam 40%, sand 20%. (8) Remove flower buds every three years.

42. (1) Elaeagnus. (*E. multiflora* Thunb.) (2) Twice a day in spring and autumn. Three to four times daily in summer. Do not let the plant dry out. (3) Once a month in March-June, and Sept. (4)-(6) Same as in **41**. (7) Red loam 40%, *kanuma-tsuchi* 20%, leaf mold 20%, sand 20%. (8) Keep in warm place in winter.

43. (1) Loquat. (*Eriobotrya japonica* Lindl.) (2) Water sparingly. (3) Once a month in March, April, Sept., Oct. (4) Same as in **41**. (5) July. Branch hanging. (6) Yearly in March or Sept. (7) Red loam 60%, *kuropoka* 20%, sand 20%. (8) Same as in **42**.

44. (1) Sand pear. (*Pyrus simonii* Carr.) (2) Water sparingly until tree bears fruit, then sufficiently. (3) Same as in **43**. (4) Same as in **41**. (5) June. (6) Annually in March. (7) Red loam 50%, *kuropoka* 30%, sand 20%. (8) Leave about 60% to 70% of old pot soil when transplanting.

45. (1) Persimmon. (*Diospyros kaki* L. fil.) (2) Normal. (3) Same as in **43**. (4) Nip unnecessary sprouts whenever they grow. Prune branches when transplanting. (5) June, Branch hanging. (6) Annually in April. (7) *Kuropoka* 40%, red loam 40%, sand 20%. (8) Take steps every three years to ensure the tree does not bear fruit.

46. (1) Five-leaf akebia. (*A. quinata* Decne.) (2) Sufficiently. Leaf-water in summer. (3) Once a month in March-July. (4) Nip unnecessary sprouts. (5) June. Branch hanging. (6) Annually in April. (7) Black loam 40%, red loam 30%, sand 20%, leaf mold 10%. (8) Avoid wind.

47. (1) English holly; Fine-tooth holly; Seibold ilex. (*I. serrata* Thunb. var. *sieboldii* Loes.) (2) Never allow the plant to dry out. (3) Once a month in spring and autumn. (4) Nip unnecessary sprouts before July. Prune branches when transplanting. (5) June. Cover wire with paper. (6) Annually in March. (7) Black loam 70%, red loam 30%.

48. (1) Kumquat. (*F. japonica* Swingl. var. *margarita* Makino.) (2) Normal. Avoid afternoon summer sun. (3) Once a month in Sept.–Oct. (4) Shorten unnecessary sprouts in June. Prune branches after fruit drops. (5), (6) Same as in **47.** (7) Red loam 50%, black loam 30%, sand 20%. (8) Protect from the cold in winter.

49. (1) Weeping willow; Babylon weeping willow. (*Salix babylonica* L.) (2) Never get the plant dry. Avoid afternoon summer sun. (3) Once or twice a month during March-Sept. period. (4) Prune branches when transplanting. (5) March. Hanging or wiring, but cover wire with paper (6) Twice a year in March, July. (7) *Kuropoka* 30%, *kanuma-tsuchi* 30%, red loam 20%, sand 20%. (8) Tends to weaken during winter.

50. (1) Cycad. (*Cycas revoluta* Thunb.) (2) Water sparingly. Expose to night dew. (3) Once a month in March-Sept. (4) Nip old leaves in June. (5) Bend leaf tips down with weighted string. (6) Every one or two years in March. (7) Red loam 60%, black loam 20%, sand 20%. (8) Keep indoors in winter.

Glossary

aburakasu oil cake
akatsuchi red loam
araki material for bonsai
arakida-tsuchi soil found at the bottom of rice paddy field.
bankan curving trunk
chokkan straight trunk
chuwatari name of old Chinese bonsai vessel (not older than *kowatari*)
daiki rootstock
dohimo bonsai vessel name
eda-zashi branch-cutting
fukuroshiki bonsai vessel name
futokoro-eda bonsai vessel name
fuyodo leaf mold
gakuiri bonsai vessel name
gobo-ne taproot
goro-tsuchi large-grained soil
hazashi leaf-cutting
hamizu leaf-watering
hariganekake wiring
hige-ne ciliary roots
honbachi real bonsai container
ishi-zuki tree with stone
jobuna bonsai vessel name
kabudachi trees in group

kabuwake separation of roots
kannuki-eda branch that must be cut because it is unsightly.
kanuma-tsuchi light clay and sand
kengai drooping trunk
keto-tsuchi peat
kowatari name of old Chinese bonsai vessel
kumoashi bonsai vessel name
kuropoka soft, blackish and slightly viscous granular soil containing a fair amount of fertilizing elements and having the ability to hold a good quantity of water.
kuro-tsuchi black loam
kuruma-eda branch that must be cut because it is unsightly.
mizugoke sphagna
misho seedage
mokko bonsai vessel name
moto-tsugi bottom grafting
naze-kaku bonsai vessel name
netsuranari separate trunks from one root
ne-zashi root-cutting
rinkashiki bonsai vessel name
sashi-ho cutting
sashiki planting a cutting
seishi training

119

sentei pruning
shakan leaning trunk
shinme-zashi sprout-cutting
shinwatari name of old Chinese bonsai vessel (not older than *chuwatari*)
sokan double trunk
sotoen bonsai vessel name
suiban shallow flower basin which does not have a small drainage hole in its bottom.
suiseki natural stone or rock with markings symbolizing mountains and gorges, or that which has patterns similar to flower petals is highly valued. Placed generally in a shallow flower basin.

sumi-iri bonsai vessel name
tekishin sprout nipping
tenjingawa-suna a kind of river sand
ten-tsugi top grafting
tochoshi excessively-grown branch
toriki layering
tsugiho scion
tsugiki grafting
uchien bonsai vessel name
udei dark grayish color including drab
yamadori collecting from a natural environment
yose-ue collective planting